W9-BGR-224

Taos Recipe

A Cookbook of Recipes from Restaurants in Taos, New Mexico

by
Joan Stromquist and Carl Stromquist

 **Tierra Publications**

Copyright © 1990 by Tierra Publications

All rights reserved. No part of this book may be
reproduced in any form, or by any means, except
for brief reviews, without the written permission
of the publisher.

Tierra Publications
2801 Rodeo Road
Suite B-612
Santa Fe, New Mexico 87505

Additional copies may be obtained by contacting
Tierra Publications. For your convenience, order
forms are included in the back of the book.

Cover design by James Finnell
Chama Graphics
Santa Fe, New Mexico

Photographs by Mark Nohl
Santa Fe, New Mexico

Library of Congress Catalog Card Number:
89-51992

ISBN: 0-9622807-1-2

Printed in the United States of America

Taos Plaza

Acknowledgement

This book is dedicated to the talented chefs and restaurant owners of Taos. We appreciate their generosity in providing us with these outstanding recipes.

Photography

The photographs in this book are the work of award-winning Mark Nohl, a native of Santa Fe. Mark has been with the New Mexico Tourism and Travel Division as staff photographer since 1973, promoting the state through his beautiful photographs of its scenic wonders. His work appears in numerous magazines, both in the United States and Europe, as well as in galleries and art shows across the country.

Cover Art

The talented James Finnell of Chama Graphics is both a free-lance illustrator and a fine artist. With 25 years of experience, he has worked on many national accounts, such as Continental Airlines, Nissan, Parker Brothers, and Mattel. Jim's favorite subject matter for painting is locomotives, and he is well-known among the nation's train buffs. Recently his interest in portraying mechanical subjects has expanded to include exotic cars, and his reputation is growing in this area as well.

Special Note

For those of you who may not have access to some of the Southwestern ingredients mentioned in these recipes, we have made arrangements with several Santa Fe businesses to supply these items through their mail order services. Please see Supplemental Information on page 172 for their addresses and phone numbers.

Joan and Carl Stromquist
Santa Fe, New Mexico

Table of Contents

Food Categories

*"You cannot come to Taos . . . without feeling
that here is one of the chosen spots on earth."*

D.H. Lawrence

Ornamental Lamp and Chile Ristra, Taos, New Mexico

Appletree

One of the most beloved and popular restaurants in Taos, the Appletree serves marvelous dishes that are prepared with the freshest ingredients possible. Here diners can relax in the courtyard under the wonderful old apple tree, knowing that an excellent meal awaits them!

Menu

*Chilled Strawberry
Pecan Soup*

Michelle's Minestrone

*Appletree Sesame Tamari
Salad Dressing*

*Creamy Chicken
Pequin Pasta*

Shrimp Sauté Mexicali

*Grilled Salmon
with Eggplant Tempura
Cucumber-Dill Sauce*

*Marinated Shrimp and
Scallop Brochette
Teriyaki Sauce*

*Teriyaki Tofu and
Steamed Vegetables
Satay Sauce*

*Walnut Torte
Mocha Buttercream Frosting*

Owner Ginny Greeno credits this recipe to Tom Mally, a chef who loves to use nuts in cold soups. She says, *"It's nice, light, and refreshing!"*

Chilled Strawberry Pecan Soup

2	cups plain yogurt
2	cups apple juice
1	cup sour cream
½	cup honey
1½	ounces strawberry liqueur
2	pints strawberries, cleaned, cored, and quartered
½	cup pecans, finely chopped
½	cup whole pecans
6	sprigs mint

In a large blender place the yogurt, apple juice, sour cream, honey, and strawberry liqueur. Purée the ingredients.

In a food processor place ½ of the strawberries and purée them. Add the purée to the mixture in the blender.

Add the chopped pecans to the blender.

Purée the mixture.

Pour the puréed soup into a large serving bowl. Add the remainder of the strawberries and the whole pecans, and stir them in.

Garnish the soup with the mint sprigs.

serves 6

Michelle's Minestrone

1½	cups dried navy beans, washed
9	cups water
3	medium carrots, chopped
1	pound Italian sausage links
3	cloves garlic, minced
2	medium onions, chopped
5	stalks celery, chopped
3	medium zucchini, chopped
4	tablespoons dried basil
½	teaspoon ground sage
1	bunch parsley, minced
2	16-ounce cans tomatoes, chopped
2	teaspoons salt
2	teaspoons black pepper
1½	cups elbow macaroni, cooked al dente

In a large, heavy kettle place the beans, water, and carrots. Bring the liquid to a boil. Cover the pot and simmer the beans for 2 to 3 hours.

In a large skillet place the sausage and fry it on medium heat until it is well cooked. Remove the sausage and set it aside. Leave the drippings in the skillet.

In the same skillet *(with the drippings)* add the garlic, onions, celery, zucchini, basil, sage, and parsley. Sauté the vegetables on medium high heat until the onions are transparent.

Add the sautéed vegetables, chopped tomatoes, salt, and pepper to the soup.

Chop the sausage and add it to the soup.

Simmer the soup for 1 more hour.

Add the elbow macaroni and stir it in.

serves 8

"Michelle Mechling is the designer of this recipe. One of our customers was an upscale man from New York City who was used to eating in very exclusive Italian restaurants. He told us that this was the best minestrone he had ever eaten, which was quite a compliment!"

"Our local clientele loves hearty soups like this. A bowl of this soup, and a thick slice of some good homemade bread, and a nice green salad.....you have a complete meal! And, when you leave the table, you feel great."

"There is a wonderful team spirit to the people who work in our restaurant, which I think makes us special."

Appletree Sesame Tamari Salad Dressing

3	cloves garlic, minced
½	cup lemon juice, freshly squeezed
¼	cup tamari *(or soy sauce)*
⅔	cup salad oil
2	tablespoons sesame oil
⅓	cup tahini
2	tablespoons sesame seeds
1	teaspoon parsley, minced

In a medium bowl place all of the ingredients and beat them together until they are well mixed.

makes 2 cups

"This is probably the oldest recipe at the Appletree. People just love it and they will come back to our restaurant year after year to enjoy it on our salads."

"The dressing freezes very well if you want to make larger batches of it."

"This dressing is excellent as a dip for raw vegetables at a party. Also, you can thin it down with some lemon juice and then use it as a marinade."

Creamy Chicken Pequin Pasta

3	tablespoons clarified butter
2	chicken breasts, skin removed, boned, and diced into ¾" cubes
½	pound mushrooms, sliced
¼	cup pimientos, sliced
¼	cup black olives, sliced
1	tablespoon garlic, minced
1	tablespoon pequin *(crushed red peppers)*
⅓	cup Marsala
1	cup heavy cream
1	pound linguini, cooked al dente
¼	cup Parmesan cheese, freshly grated
2	tablespoons green onions, chopped

In an extra large skillet place the clarified butter and heat it on medium high until it is hot.

Add the chicken pieces and sauté them for 2 to 3 minutes, or until they just start to turn brown.

Add the mushrooms, pimientos, olives, garlic, and pequin. Sauté the ingredients for 1 to 2 minutes, or until the mushrooms are tender.

Add the Marsala and deglaze the pan. Cook the sauce for 1 minute.

Add the heavy cream and stir it in. Cook the sauce for 1 to 2 minutes, or until it is thickened.

Serve the sauce over the linguini.

Sprinkle on the Parmesan cheese and green onions.

serves 4

"Lori Frech, one of our chefs, is really wonderful with sauces, particularly with rich sauces. This is one of the dishes she has come up with that we all really like."

"Use any kind of mushrooms that you want, but local wild mushrooms will make it really special."

"Play with the amount of pequin. If your family likes hot things, then you probably could use a lot more. Also, you can add some fresh chopped green chiles to the green onions that you sprinkle on top."

Shrimp Sauté Mexicali

"This is another recipe that Lori Frech created. She likes to take ideas from different sources and then mingle them together."

3	tablespoons olive oil
½	cup tomatoes, chopped
⅓	cup green bell peppers, chopped
⅓	cup red onions, chopped
¼	cup black olives, sliced
¼	cup green olives, sliced
1	tablespoon garlic, minced
2	tablespoons jalapeño peppers, seeded and minced
3	tablespoons dried currants
⅛	teaspoon ground cloves
⅛	teaspoon ground cinnamon
⅛	teaspoon cayenne pepper
½	teaspoon pequin *(crushed red peppers)*
½	teaspoon cumin
½	teaspoon ground coriander
	salt *(to taste)*
	pepper *(to taste)*
1½	pounds large shrimp, shelled and deveined
¼	cup Madeira
⅓	cup orange juice
2	tablespoons butter
4	cups cooked white rice
¼	cup slivered almonds, toasted

"The dish is not spicy with the amount of jalapeño and cayenne pepper called for. Of course, you certainly can up the amount!"

In a large skillet place the olive oil and heat it on medium high until it is hot.

Add the tomatoes, bell peppers, red onions, black olives, green olives, garlic, jalapeño peppers, currants, cloves, cinnamon, cayenne pepper, pequin, cumin, coriander, salt, and pepper. Mix the ingredients together and sauté them for 2 to 3 minutes.

Add the shrimp and sauté them until they just start to turn pink.

"We all love this recipe. It's healthy, simple to make, and tastes wonderful!"

Add the Madeira and orange juice, and deglaze the pan. Cook the ingredients for 1 to 2 minutes, or until the liquid is reduced by ½.

Add the butter and swirl it in so that the sauce thickens.

Serve the shrimp over the white rice. Garnish the dish with the almonds.

serves 4-6

Grilled Salmon with Eggplant Tempura and Cucumber-Dill Sauce

Grilled Salmon with Eggplant Tempura

1	clove garlic, minced
¾	cup balsamic vinegar
¼	cup lemon juice
1	teaspoon salt
1	teaspoon white pepper
2	cups olive oil
1	large eggplant, cut into ½" medallions
½	cup flour
1	cup vegetable oil
	Tempura Batter *(recipe on next page)*
4	7-ounce salmon fillets
	Cucumber-Dill Sauce *(recipe on next page)*

In a large bowl place the garlic, vinegar, lemon juice, salt, and white pepper. Mix everything together well.

While whisking constantly, add the olive oil in a slow, steady stream.

Add the eggplant medallions and coat them well.

Cover the medallions and refrigerate them for 2 hours. Turn them occasionally.

Remove the medallions and drain them. Dredge them in the flour so that they are well-coated.

In a large skillet place the vegetable oil and heat it on medium high until it is hot. Dip the eggplant medallions in the batter and fry them for 1 to 2 minutes on each side, or until they are golden brown. Drain them on paper towels.

Grill the salmon for 5 to 7 minutes, or until it is just done *(do not overcook)*.

Place 2 eggplant medallions on each individual serving plate. Place the salmon fillet on top. Spoon the Cucumber-Dill Sauce over the fish. *(Note: Cucumber-Dill Sauce must be made at least 2 hours before serving.)*

serves 4

"Tracy Manning is the chef who came up with this recipe. We love marinating foods in our restaurant, and this is an especially good example of a nice marinade. The eggplant really acquires an unusual taste, plus it gets tenderized."

"There is a very interesting combination of flavors and textures in this dish. Try it!"

"The Appletree will be doing its own cookbook in the near future. The proceeds will go to a local charity."

Tempura Batter

4	eggs
2	cups flour
1	teaspoon baking powder
½	teaspoon salt
1	teaspoon sugar
18	ounces strong, dark beer

In a large bowl place all of the ingredients and mix them together until they are well blended.

"You can use this recipe for tempura shrimp, fish, or vegetables."

Cucumber-Dill Sauce

1	medium cucumber, peeled, seeded, and diced into ¼" cubes
2	cups sour cream
1	cup fresh dill, minced
2	tablespoons fresh chives
1	tablespoon Dijon mustard
½	teaspoon champagne vinegar

In a medium bowl place all of the ingredients.

Whisk them together for 3 to 4 minutes.

Cover the bowl tightly and refrigerate the sauce for 2 hours.

Remove the sauce 10 minutes before serving, so that it is slightly chilled.

"The Cucumber-Dill Sauce is amazing! And, it works well on a lot of different things..... especially other kinds of fish. It also is excellent with deep-fried vegetables, such as zucchini."

"We have a woman on our staff who grows fresh herbs for us, and I think that an abundance of dill was the inspiration for this recipe."

"Be sure that you seed the cucumber. And don't cut it too small. It should be diced into little chunks."

Marinated Shrimp and Scallop Brochette with Teriyaki Sauce

Marinated Shrimp and Scallop Brochette

1½	pounds medium shrimp, shelled and deveined
1	pound sea scallops
2	red onions, cut into wedges
2	red bell peppers, cut into 1" squares
2	tomatoes, cut into wedges
5	shitake mushrooms, cut in half
1	12-ounce bottle dark ale
½	cup sesame oil
2	limes, juiced and zested *(outer green part grated off)*
1	1" piece fresh ginger, peeled and chopped
2	cloves garlic, peeled and crushed
2	tablespoons soy sauce
¼	cup fresh cilantro, chopped
1	dash salt
1	dash pepper
3	cups white rice, cooked
	Teriyaki Sauce *(recipe on next page)*

On 12 skewers place *(in an alternating order)* the shrimp, scallops, onions, peppers, tomatoes, and mushrooms.

In a large, shallow dish place the ale, sesame oil, lime juice, lime zest, ginger, garlic, soy sauce, cilantro, salt and pepper. Mix the ingredients together.

Place the brochettes in the marinade and let them soak for 8 hours. Turn the skewers occasionally.

Grill the brochettes for 3 minutes on each side.

Serve the brochettes with the white rice and a side dish of the Teriyaki Sauce.

serves 6

"Pam Chappell is another of our chefs who is excellent with marinades, and this is one of her recipes."

"This is really a nice dish! You can rush the marinade if necessary, and do it for two hours. However, the longer the ingredients sit in the marinade the better and better they get, up to about eight hours. After that, it's probably pointless."

"People who are watching their weight will especially love this dish!"

"This looks very pretty on the plate. Serve it with your favorite kind of rice."

Teriyaki Sauce

2	cloves garlic
1	1" piece fresh ginger, peeled
2	tablespoons sesame oil
1	cup sherry
2	tablespoons sugar
1½	teaspoons ground coriander
¼	teaspoon cumin
⅓	cup soy sauce
3	cups pineapple juice

In a food processor place the garlic and ginger. Purée them until they are a fine consistency.

In a medium saucepan place the oil and heat it on medium until it is hot. Add the puréed garlic and ginger, and sauté them for 1 minute.

Add the sherry and bring it to a boil. Reduce the heat and simmer the ingredients until the liquid is reduced by ½.

Add the sugar, coriander, cumin, soy sauce, and pineapple juice. Simmer the sauce for 1 hour.

"You can buy teriyaki sauce in a bottle, but this recipe is much nicer. Also, you don't have to worry about MSG, because you have complete control over what goes into it. Instead of the soy sauce you can use tamari, or even wheat-free tamari."

"We are feeding a lot of people in our restaurant and we feel a strong responsibility to feed them well. We use the freshest ingredients possible, and we treat the food properly.....with respect. We call this 'food ethics'."

Teriyaki Tofu and Steamed Vegetables with Satay Sauce

Teriyaki Tofu and Steamed Vegetables

2   cups Teriyaki Sauce *(recipe on previous page)*
1   block firm tofu, drained and cubed
8   cups fresh vegetables, steamed
4   cups cooked white rice
    Satay Sauce *(recipe on next page)*

In a medium saucepan place the Teriyaki Sauce and bring it to a boil. Place the tofu cubes in the sauce, bring the liquid to a boil, and then remove the tofu with a slotted spoon.

On individual serving plates place the white rice. Spoon the tofu and steamed vegetables on top.

Serve a small dish of the Satay Sauce on the side.

serves 6

"This is one of the few dishes that we have served for many, many years. It's also one of the few recipes that we haven't changed at all over time."

"Our restaurant is organized a little differently from most others in that we do not have one head chef. Rather, we have a team of chefs who come from diverse backgrounds. Each noon and night a different chef is in charge, and he or she can create whatever he or she desires. The underlying factor is that they all are very committed to making dishes with the best and freshest ingredients that they can find, and then serving the food in the most interesting ways that they can dream up. We are very fortunate to have the talent that we do at this restaurant."

Satay Sauce

1	red onion, chopped
1	1" piece ginger root, peeled and chopped
1	clove garlic
⅓	cup sesame oil
3	tablespoons red wine vinegar
3	tablespoons brown sugar
2	cups water, hot
1	cup peanut butter
½	cup catsup
½	cup soy sauce
1½	teaspoons ground coriander
1½	teaspoons black pepper
½	teaspoon tabasco

In a food processor place the onions, ginger, and garlic. Purée the ingredients until they are smooth.

In a large skillet place the oil and heat it on medium until it is hot. Add the puréed onion mixture and sauté it for 1 minute.

In a medium saucepan place the red wine vinegar and brown sugar. Heat the mixture until the sugar caramelizes. Remove it from the heat and add it to the sautéed onions.

Add the hot water, peanut butter, catsup, soy sauce, coriander, pepper, and tabasco. Stir the ingredients together and simmer them for 5 minutes.

"The Satay Sauce is wonderful! It also makes a delicious marinade, especially for meats. Just thin it down some with a little water, lemon juice, or vinegar."

"Our clientele is very diverse, ranging from locals who eat here all the time, to visitors who need to have everything explained to them in great detail."

Walnut Torte
with Mocha Buttercream Frosting

Walnut Torte

2½ cups flour
1¾ teaspoons baking powder
1   pinch salt
1   cup walnuts, ground
1½ cups heavy cream
5   eggs
1⅓ cups sugar
1   tablespoon vanilla
    Mocha Buttercream Frosting (recipe on next page)

In a medium bowl sift together the flour, baking powder, and salt.

Add the ground walnuts and stir them in.

In a small bowl place the heavy cream and beat it until it is not quite stiff (soft peaks are formed). Refrigerate the whipped cream.

In a large bowl place the eggs and sugar. Beat them for 5 to 7 minutes, or until they form a ribbon.

Add the vanilla and fold it in.

Add the dry ingredients and fold them in.

Add the whipped cream and fold it in.

Preheat the oven to 350°.

Pour the batter into two 9" greased and floured cake pans.

Bake the layers for 12 to 15 minutes, or until the tops are golden brown and a toothpick inserted comes out clean.

Let the layers cool.

Slice them in half, horizontally, so that there are 4 layers.

Frost each layer with the Mocha Buttercream Frosting, and stack them. Frost the outside of the torte. Use any extra frosting for decorations.

serves 12

"Carol Duesbury, the creator of this recipe, is a very accomplished weaving and tapestry artist. And, she has carried her artistic talent over to making desserts. She is truly a gifted person, and her desserts are excellent!"

"This recipe is complicated, but well worth the effort. It makes a startling dessert, both visually and taste-wise."

"Try sprinkling grated semi-sweet chocolate on top of the butter cream for each layer."

"Try melting some semi-sweet chocolate and swirling it into the frosting on top. The combination of mocha and chocolate is irresistible!"

"Don't be tempted to speed the process by adding the butter before the egg-syrup mixture has cooled. Otherwise, the buttercream will become runny and foamy instead of light and fluffy."

"The name of the restaurant came from the huge apple tree growing in the courtyard. No one is sure what the variety is. Or, if they do know, they aren't willing to speak up! We use the apples, when there are enough of them, to make apple pies for what we call 'free apple pie day'. This is a day when, after most of the tourists are gone, everyone in the town is invited to come over and have free apple pie. This is a tradition that was started by Polly Raye, the previous owner."

Mocha Buttercream Frosting

1⅛	cups sugar
⅜	cup water
8	egg yolks
1	pound butter, cut into 1" cubes
2¼	tablespoons instant coffee, dissolved in 1 tablespoon hot water
2	tablespoons Kahlua

In a small saucepan place the sugar and water and heat them on medium until the sugar melts. Raise the heat and boil the syrup until it reaches 250°. Remove it from the heat.

While the syrup is boiling, place the egg yolks in a medium bowl and beat them until they turn pale and a ribbon forms.

While continuing to beat the egg yolks on a high speed, slowly add the syrup. Continue to beat the mixture for 10 to 15 minutes, or until it cools.

While continuing to beat the mixture, drop in the cubes of butter, one at a time.

Drizzle in the coffee and the Kahlua, and lightly mix them in.

Adobe Wall Detail, Ranchos de Taos, New Mexico

Austing Haus

Elegant, light, and airy, the Austing Haus offers spectacular mountain views as well as an excellent classical cuisine in its *Glass Dining Room*. This is one restaurant where, if the dish doesn't look like a picture perfect photograph, it doesn't leave the kitchen!

Menu

French Onion Soup
Potatoes Lyonaise
Fettucini Alfredo
Shrimp Scampi
Veal Stephan
Bordelaise Sauce
Steak au Poivre
Baked Alaska

Owner, builder, and chef, Paul Austing, was trained in classical cuisine, and he loves to cook in the classical way.

"This onion soup is a very simple, classic recipe. The key to the good flavor is to cook the onions long enough so that they get lightly browned. Don't be afraid of overcooking them."

French Onion Soup

1 tablespoon butter
4 medium onions, sliced
8 cups beef broth
1 tablespoon brandy
½ teaspoon Worcestershire sauce
⅛ teaspoon garlic powder
   salt *(to taste)*
   pepper *(to taste)*
4 large croutons
2 tablespoons Parmesan cheese, freshly grated

In a medium saucepan place the butter and heat it on medium until it has melted. Add the onions and sauté them for 10 to 15 minutes, or until they are clear and lightly browned.

Add the beef broth, brandy, Worcestershire sauce, garlic powder, salt, and pepper. Simmer the soup for 20 minutes.

Ladle the soup into individual oven-proof serving bowls. Place one crouton on top of each bowl of soup and sprinkle on some of the Parmesan cheese.

In a preheated oven broil the soup until the cheese browns.

serves 4

Potatoes Lyonaise

2   **large Idaho potatoes, peeled and sliced ¼" thick**
¼   **cup onions, diced**
¼   **cup green bell peppers, diced**
⅛   **cup pimientos, chopped**
       paprika *(to taste)*
       salt *(to taste)*
       pepper *(to taste)*
3   **tablespoons butter, melted**

In a small shallow baking dish lay the potato slices in rows.

Sprinkle on the onions, bell peppers, and pimientos.

Dust the potatoes with the paprika, salt, and pepper.

Lace the potatoes with the butter.

Preheat the oven to 375˚. Cover the potatoes and bake them for 30 minutes, or until they are done.

serves 4

"This is an excellent recipe and it tastes wonderful! It's very easy to make, and just like most of our dishes, the key to its success lies in its presentation. There is the strong contrast of colors with the red, green, and white, which is important to the appearance of the dish. Also, this potato dish is not that common, and it looks a lot more difficult to make than it really is."

Fettucini Alfredo

1   **pound egg fettucini noodles, cooked al dente**
1½   **cups heavy cream**
¾   **cup Parmesan cheese, freshly grated**
       pepper *(to taste)*
2   **lemons, quartered**

In an extra large skillet place the fettucini, heavy cream, Parmesan cheese, and pepper. Heat the ingredients on medium and stir them until the sauce is thick and creamy, and the pasta is well coated.

Serve the pasta immediately. Garnish it with the lemon wedges.

serves 4

"Make certain that the noodles are firm to the bite when you quit boiling them, because they will be cooking longer in the sauce."

"I recommend that you cook this dish in a teflon pan, which will prevent the ingredients from sticking to it. Again, this is a very simple dish and very easy to make. But then, I believe that most good cooking is very simple."

"It's important not to cook this dish too long, or else you will end up with a thick blob! Also, don't cook it too little or it will be like a soup."

"Shrimp scampi can be done in a variety of ways. The key thing is that it must be served with a garlic butter sauce. Because I personally hate to go to a restaurant and then have to wrestle with my food, we peel the shrimp in this recipe. The tails are left on so that you can hold the shrimp and eat them with your fingers. Or, you can eat them with a fork."

"When you slice the shrimp down the center, be sure that you don't slice too far. And, if you lay your shrimp out in a haphazard way, then your plate won't look very attractive. So, make sure that the cut side is facing up, that the tails are up, and that they are attractively fanned out."

Shrimp Scampi

20	large shrimp, shelled and deveined, with tails left on
2	tablespoons garlic, minced
2	tablespoons bread crumbs
½	pound butter, clarified
1	lemon, quartered

Slice the shrimp lengthwise, down the center of the underside, to the edge of the tail. Fold them open.

In each of 4 individual casserole dishes place 5 of the shrimp in a fan-like pattern, with the tails and the split sides facing upwards.

Sprinkle ½ tablespoon of the garlic on each serving.

Sprinkle ½ tablespoon of the bread crumbs on each serving.

Lace the butter over the top.

Preheat the oven to 450° and bake the shrimp for 10 minutes, or until they are lightly browned.

Garnish the shrimp with the lemon wedges.

serves 4

Veal Stephan

1	**egg**
¼	**cup milk**
1¼	**pounds veal medallions, pounded to ⅛" thick**
¼	**cup flour**
½	**pound butter, clarified**
½	**pound mushrooms, thinly sliced**
1	**cup white wine**
1	**cup Bordelaise Sauce** *(recipe on next page)*
1	**lemon, quartered**

In a small bowl place the egg and milk, and mix them together well.

Coat the veal medallions with the flour. Dip them in the egg wash. Coat them again with the flour.

In a large skillet place the butter and heat it on medium high until it is hot. Sauté the coated veal medallions for 3 to 4 minutes on each side, or until they are golden brown. Remove the medallions and set them aside.

Add the mushrooms to the skillet and sauté them for 1 minute.

Add the wine and the Bordelaise Sauce. Cook the ingredients for 5 to 7 minutes, or until the sauce is slightly thickened and creamy. Stir the sauce occasionally.

Pour the sauce over the medallions. Garnish them with the lemon wedges.

serves 4

"This is a classic recipe that was named after a Swiss chef – Stephan. Many of the classic dishes are named after famous people or the chefs who developed them."

"The key to the success of this recipe lies in the consistency of the sauce. Cook it long enough to get rid of the bitterness of the white wine. This should be a light, elegant dish. It is not heavy, even though it is very rich and filling. It looks dainty on the plate, not thick like a steak, although when you leave the table you will be full."

"Snow peas are a wonderful vegetable to serve with this dish. We steam them until they are al dente. They add a tremendous amount of character to the plate, and they are very economical to serve, even though they cost a lot per pound. Look at the cost per serving, not the cost per pound. In this case snow peas are much more economical to serve than broccoli or cauliflower."

"Don't use a cheap burgundy wine when you make this sauce.....use a good one. My two secrets to good cooking are butter and booze. I never use a cheap alcoholic beverage.....I always use the best possible. You only use a small quantity, and a good, high quality brand will make ALL the difference in the way your dish or sauce tastes!"

"You can use beef base to make the consommé, or you can buy it in a can in the store. And never, never add salt!"

"Your basic brown sauce is only going to be as good as your stock. Now, most people don't have time to make a really good, traditional stock. So, I recommend that you go to your favorite grocery store and pick up the Knorr products, which are incredible! They come from Switzerland, and one thing about the Swiss is that they never cheat..... they always go first class! Just follow the directions and you will end up with a perfect sauce every time."

Bordelaise Sauce

2	teaspoons butter
2	teaspoons shallots, minced
1	tablespoon butter
1	tablespoon flour
1½	cups beef consommé, heated
¼	cup burgundy wine

In a small saucepan place the 2 teaspoons of butter and heat it on medium high until it has melted. Add the shallots and sauté them for 2 to 3 minutes. Set them aside.

In a medium saucepan place the 1 tablespoon of butter and heat it on medium until it has melted.

Add the flour and stir it for 1 minute.

While whisking constantly, slowly add the heated beef consommé. Make certain that no lumps form.

Add the shallots and wine, and stir them in.

Simmer the sauce for 10 minutes, or until it has reached a creamy consistency.

Steak au Poivre

4	10-ounce New York strip steaks
½	pound mushrooms, thickly sliced
1½	cups Bordelaise Sauce *(recipe on previous page)*
1½	ounces brandy
2	tablespoons green peppercorns

Heat an extra large skillet on high. Hold 2 of the steaks in your hands and place them in the pan on their edges, with the fat side down. Hold them there until some of the fat melts off, so that the pan is nicely greased.

Cook the steaks on each side until slightly less than the desired doneness is achieved. Remove the steaks from the pan and set them aside. Repeat the process for the remaining 2 steaks.

Add the mushrooms, Bordelaise Sauce, brandy, and green peppercorns to the skillet. Stir the ingredients together well. Cook the sauce for 3 minutes.

Place the steaks back in the skillet, and simmer them for 3 to 4 minutes. Serve the steaks immediately.

serves 4

"Steak au Poivre is another classical recipe. You can use either a New York strip or a filet. If you do use the filet then you should add a little butter when you cook it. But with strips, no extra grease or butter is necessary."

"I believe that you eat with your eyes first, then with your nose, and finally with your mouth. If the food looks wonderful to your eyes then the message will go to your brain that it will taste just as wonderful as it looks. Something can taste very, very good, but if it is presented poorly, then psychologically the person already will have been turned off. So, the appearance of a dish is a very important factor to me. In fact, I personally inspect every single dish that comes out of our kitchen. Each one must be picture perfect!"

"To make a Baked Alaska you need a sponge or pound cake, ice cream, and meringue. Now, with these three ingredients you can add different kinds of liqueurs, ice cream, fruits, or whatever. And, you should spend some time adding little decorations with the meringue. This will make the presentation very elegant. A beautiful appearance is the key in a nice Baked Alaska."

"When you are baking this in the oven keep a close eye on it, because for a long while the meringue won't appear to be doing anything, and then all of a sudden it will turn brown. Remove it immediately.....you can ruin it really fast!"

"A beautiful presentation will make the most simple dish seem exciting and difficult to make."

Baked Alaska

1	small pound cake
8	ounces vanilla ice cream
3	tablespoons Grand Marnier
4	medium egg whites
⅓	cup sugar

From the top of the cake, cut out and remove a 1¼" square channel, lengthwise, down the center *(the channel should run down the full length of the cake)*.

Fill the channel with the ice cream.

Place the removed piece of cake on top of the ice cream. Slowly pour the Grand Marnier on top of the strip of cake.

Place the cake in the freezer.

In a small bowl place the egg whites. Beat them on high speed with an electric mixer until they are fluffy and creamy *(do not form peaks)*.

Continue beating the egg whites and slowly add the sugar. Beat them until the meringue is thick and heavy, and stiff peaks are formed.

Remove the cake from the freezer.

Artfully spread the meringue on the cake.

Preheat the oven to 400°. Bake the cake for 3 to 4 minutes, or until the meringue is lightly browned.

serves 4

Bell Tower, St. Francis de Asisi Church, Ranchos de Taos, New Mexico

Brett House

Customers who dine at the Brett House can enjoy its fresh and original cuisine in the pleasant ambiance of an elegant old adobe home. The sweeping views of the Sangre de Cristo mountains are the perfect complement to a memorable dining experience in this well-respected restaurant.

Brett House Salad
with Walnut Oil Vinaigrette

Brett House Salad

4   **leaves radicchio, washed and dried**
4   **sprigs arugala, washed and dried**
1   **head Boston Bibb lettuce, washed, dried, and torn**
     Walnut Oil Vinaigrette *(recipe on next page)*
2   **tablespoons walnut pieces**

On 4 individual salad plates place a leaf of the radicchio and a sprig of the arugala.

Place the torn Boston Bibb lettuce pieces on top.

Sprinkle on the Walnut Oil Vinaigrette.

Sprinkle on the walnut pieces.

serves 4

Menu

Brett House Salad
Walnut Oil Vinaigrette

Brett House Black
Bean Soup

Spinach Fettucini with
Sun-Dried Tomatoes
and Goat Cheese

Catfish in Cornmeal
Maître d'Butter

Chicken Breast Roulade
with Chorizo
Red Chile Sauce

Lobster Terrine
Cilantro Champagne Cream

Frozen Lemon Ribbon Torte
Vanilla Sauce

Chuck Lamendola is both a part-owner and the chef of the popular Brett House Restaurant.

"This is a very basic salad using different kinds of greens. The radicchio is slightly bitter and the arugala is lemony."

Walnut Oil Vinaigrette

4	tablespoons Dijon mustard
1	tablespoon fresh basil, minced
1	teaspoon garlic, minced
1	teaspoon shallots, minced
2	teaspoons powdered sugar
¼	cup balsamic vinegar
¼	cup red wine vinegar
1	cup walnut oil
1	cup vegetable oil
⅛	teaspoon tabasco
⅛	teaspoon Worcestershire sauce
1	tablespoon white wine
	salt *(to taste)*
	pepper *(to taste)*

In a medium bowl place the mustard, basil, garlic, shallots, and powdered sugar. Whisk the ingredients together.

While whisking constantly, slowly add the two vinegars.

While continuing to whisk constantly, slowly dribble in the two oils.

Add the tabasco, Worcestershire sauce, and white wine. Whisk the ingredients together well.

Add the salt and pepper, and whisk them in.

"I like to use the balsamic vinegar because it has such a wonderful flavor. However, the taste is very strong, so I cut it with some red wine vinegar."

"Balsamic vinegar has been aged in oak casks in Italy. It is fairly dark in color. Please try it if you never have.....you will be happy to discover a new vinegar with such a great flavor!"

"The walnut oil has a wonderful, nutty taste. But again, you have to be careful with it because the flavor is very distinctive and powerful."

"You may use different kinds of oil if you like. Also, feel free to add other fresh herbs if you have them."

Brett House Black Bean Soup

1	pound black turtle beans, stones removed, rinsed, and soaked overnight
1	onion, chopped medium
1	carrot, chopped medium
1	stalk celery, chopped medium
6	cloves garlic, chopped
1	smoked ham hock
3	jalapeño peppers, seeds removed, and chopped
2	quarts chicken stock *(or as needed)*
1	tablespoon cumin
1	tablespoon red chile powder
1	tablespoon cayenne pepper
1½	cups sour cream
2	cups heavy cream
	salt *(to taste)*

"After the Milagro Beanfield War *movie came out, everything was 'Milagro' this and 'Milagro' that. So, my partners and I decided to make up a soup to go along with the movie, and this is it!"*

Drain the beans.

In a large, heavy saucepan place the beans, onions, carrots, celery, garlic, ham hock, jalapeño peppers, and chicken stock *(enough to cover the beans)*.

Over a high heat bring the liquid to a boil. Skim off any foam that rises to the top.

Loosely cover the pan, reduce the heat, and slowly simmer the beans for 3 hours, or until they are tender. Add more stock if necessary *(the level of liquid should not fall below the surface of the beans)*. Stir the beans often to prevent them from sticking and to ensure that they cook evenly.

"The combination of the ingredients blends really well together. The smoked ham hock gives it a great flavor, and it's not a spicy soup even though there are jalapeño peppers in it."

Remove the ham hock.

In a food processor place the soup and purée it.

Add the cumin, red chile powder, and cayenne pepper. Stir them in.

In a small bowl place the sour cream and heavy cream, and mix them together. Add the cream mixture to the soup.

Add the salt. Adjust the seasoning if necessary.

Reheat the soup before serving it.

serves 8

Spinach Fettucini with Sun-Dried Tomatoes and Goat Cheese

¼	cup olive oil
1	cup oyster mushrooms, sliced
1	tablespoon shallots, finely chopped
1	tablespoon garlic, minced
¼	cup sun-dried tomatoes *(reconstituted)*
3	tablespoons white wine
1	tablespoon fresh basil, finely chopped
1	pound spinach fettucini, cooked al dente
	salt *(to taste)*
	pepper *(to taste)*
⅛	cup goat cheese, crumbled

In an extra large skillet place the oil and heat it on medium until it is hot.

Add the mushrooms, shallots, garlic, and sun-dried tomatoes. Sauté the ingredients for 2 to 3 minutes, or until the mushrooms are slightly cooked.

Add the wine and stir it in. Cook the ingredients for 1 minute.

Add the basil and stir it in.

Add the pasta, salt, and pepper. Mix the ingredients together thoroughly so that the pasta is well coated. Add more oil if the pasta seems too dry.

Place the pasta on a serving platter. Sprinkle the goat cheese on top.

serves 4

"This is a delicious recipe and it stems from a combination of ingredients that my mother used in her restaurant when I was a young boy. It is a cross between an Italian and a Greek dish.....very Mediterranean!"

"There are different types of goat cheese, and some of them are very strong, which a lot of people aren't used to. But the Montrachet is very mild, as is the local goat cheese which we try to use here."

"If you use sun-dried tomatoes that are dry, then you have to reconstitute them. Bring them to a boil in salted water and then let them sit for five minutes. Strain them, and then store them in olive oil."

Catfish in Cornmeal with Maître d'Butter

Catfish in Cornmeal

4	**8-ounce catfish fillets**
2	**cups buttermilk**
2	**cups cornmeal**
½	**cup oil** *(or as needed)*
4	**1" pinwheels of Maître d'Butter** *(recipe follows)*

In a medium bowl place the catfish and the buttermilk. Let the fish soak at room temperature for 2 hours.

Remove the catfish and let them drain. Thoroughly coat the fish in the cornmeal.

In a large skillet place the oil and heat it on high until it is very hot. Quickly fry the fish on both sides so that they are golden brown.

Preheat the oven to 375°. Place the catfish in a pan and bake them for 10 minutes, or until they are just done.

Place one pinwheel of the Maître d'Butter on top of each fish fillet.

serves 4

Maître d'Butter

1	**pound unsalted butter, softened**
3	**jalapeño peppers, seeds removed, and finely diced**
1	**tablespoon cilantro, finely chopped**
1	**tablespoon red bell peppers, finely chopped**
1	**tablespoon yellow bell peppers, finely chopped**
1	**clove garlic, minced**
	salt *(to taste)*
	pepper *(to taste)*

In a medium bowl place all of the ingredients and cream them together.

Roll the butter up in parchment paper to form a log, and refrigerate it 30 minutes.

"Originally I was skeptical about putting catfish on our menu because I thought that people were afraid of eating it. But it has turned out to be very popular and now it's one of our best sellers. Catfish is a good, firm fish with a mild flavor."

"This is a very simple, but very flavorful recipe. By soaking the catfish in the buttermilk you get a nice tangy taste."

"When you fry the catfish you should use enough oil so that it fills your pan up to one quarter of an inch. Be sure that it is very hot so that the fish are seared and a nice crust is formed."

"The Maître d'Butter is a classic compound butter with some New Mexican flavors blended in. The pinwheel melts slightly on top of the fish and it looks really pretty."

Brett House

Chicken Breast Roulade with Chorizo and Red Chile Sauce

Chicken Breast Roulade with Chorizo

12	ounces chorizo
1	cup mushrooms, sliced
4	teaspoons fresh cilantro, minced
4	teaspoons shallots, minced
4	teaspoons garlic, minced
4	eggs
4	whole chicken breasts, skin removed, boned, and pounded *(save the skins)*
	flour *(as needed)*
4	tablespoons oil
4	tablespoons butter
	Red Chile Sauce *(recipe on next page)*
4	tablespoons sour cream

In a large skillet place the chorizo and heat it on medium high for 1 minute.

Add the mushrooms, cilantro, shallots, and garlic. Sauté the ingredients for 3 to 4 minutes, or until the mushrooms are tender.

Strain off the fat.

Place the mixture in a food processor and purée it for 10 seconds.

Add the eggs to the food processor while it is still running and purée them for 10 seconds. Let the mixture sit for 15 minutes.

Spread the mixture on each of the chicken breasts and roll them up.

Lay the 4 chicken skin pieces out flat. Place the rolled chicken breasts on top of the chicken skins with the seam sides down. Roll them up in the skins.

Lightly coat the rolled chicken with the flour.

In a large skillet place the oil and butter, and heat them on high until the butter has melted and the oil is hot. Add the rolled chicken pieces and quickly sauté them until they are lightly browned on all sides.

(continued on next page)

"When we first opened the restaurant we wanted a good chicken dish with a nice Southwestern flair. So, I got this recipe from my in-laws who live in Tucson, and then I changed it a little. The pinwheel slices look really pretty on the plate."

"We've had customers come to our restaurant specifically for this entrée, and if we were out of it they would just leave without eating! We are very well known for this particular dish."

"There are different kinds of chorizo. Some are hotter than others, and some vary in the amount of vinegar that's in them. So, if you find a brand that you like, then stick with it!"

Brett House

"Our goal at the Brett House is to make the food interesting, fresh, and flavorful. We use the best ingredients possible and make everything from scratch. We like to experiment with our dishes, but not to the point that they are too scary to eat!"

"The most important thing for this recipe is that you use a New Mexican red chile powder. If you don't, then the flavor will be totally different. The New Mexican chile powder has a very distinctive flavor. It's easy to cook with and it's not very harsh."

"When I used to cook in Detroit I would use red chile powder and it was okay, but nothing spectacular. And then when I moved to Taos and tasted this chile powder, it was like, WOW!"

Preheat the oven to 375°. Place the chicken pieces in a pan and bake them for 20 minutes, or until they are done.

Cut the rolled chicken crosswise into pinwheels.

Cover individual plates with the Red Chile Sauce. Place the pinwheels on top. Place a dollop of sour cream in the middle of the pinwheels.

serves 4

Red Chile Sauce

2	tablespoons vegetable oil
3	tablespoons flour
4	tablespoons New Mexico red chile powder
2½	cups chicken stock
2	cloves garlic, minced
1½	teaspoons salt
1	teaspoon white pepper
1½	teaspoons cumin

In a medium saucepan place the oil and heat it on medium high until it is hot. Add the flour and mix it in well.

Add the chile powder, stir it in, and cook it for 2 to 3 minutes.

Add the chicken stock and stir it in.

Add the remainder of the ingredients and stir them in.

Simmer the sauce for 15 to 20 minutes. Correct the seasoning if necessary.

Lobster Terrine
with Cilantro Champagne Cream

Lobster Terrine

1	tablespoon clarified butter
6	ounces lobster, chopped small
3	tablespoons brandy
8	ounces scallops, diced
8	ounces fresh salmon fillet, diced
2	whole eggs
1	egg white
½	cup heavy cream *(or as needed)*
¼	cup yellow bell peppers, diced
¼	cup red bell peppers, diced
3	tablespoons cilantro, chopped
2	teaspoons salt
1	teaspoon white pepper
2	dashes tabasco
1	lime, juiced
2	egg whites, beaten
	Cilantro Champagne Cream *(recipe on next page)*

In a medium skillet place the clarified butter and heat it on medium until it is hot. Add the lobster and sauté it for 2 to 3 minutes. Add the brandy and remove the skillet from the heat. Let the lobster cool to room temperature.

In a food processor place the scallops and salmon, and purée them.

While the food processor is running on low, add the eggs and the 1 egg white. Add the cream and continue blending the mixture until it is creamy in texture *(not too thin or thick)*.

Pour the mixture into a bowl. Cover the bowl, and refrigerate the mixture for 1 hour.

Add the sautéed lobster, the yellow and red bell peppers, cilantro, salt, white pepper, tabasco, and lime juice. Gently mix everything together.

Fold in the 2 beaten egg whites.

Line the bottom of a loaf pan with parchment paper. Pour in the mixture.

Place the loaf pan in a baking dish filled with 1" of hot water.

(continued on next page)

"This is the most difficult of my recipes and it's fairly time consuming. But, I believe that it is well worth the effort! It tastes wonderful and makes an elegant dish for a nice dinner party."

"This recipe was put together for a group of food editors who were touring Albuquerque, Santa Fe, and Taos. They came here for lunch and wanted to have a taste of Taos in their food. They loved it!"

"Don't over-purée the seafood mixture in the beginning. After it is puréed, then let it rest for a good half hour, so that the fish has a chance to set."

Brett House

Preheat the oven to 350°. Bake the loaf in the hot water bath for 1 to 1½ hours, or until it is firm throughout *(a knife inserted will come out clean)*.

Remove the loaf from the oven and let it sit for 10 minutes.

Remove the loaf from the pan and let it sit for 5 minutes.

Slice the loaf and serve it with the Cilantro Champagne Cream poured over the top.

serves 6

Cilantro Champagne Cream

1	**lime, juiced**
2	**ounces champagne**
2	**teaspoons cilantro, minced**
1	**teaspoon shallots, minced**
¼	**cup heavy cream**
2	**tablespoons butter**
	salt *(to taste)*
	pepper *(to taste)*

In a small saucepan place the lime juice, champagne, cilantro, and shallots.

Bring the mixture to a boil and then reduce the heat. Cook it for 1 to 2 minutes, or until the liquid is reduced.

While whisking constantly, add the heavy cream. Continue to whisk the sauce until it comes to a boil.

Add the butter, salt, and pepper. Whisk them in.

"When I was growing up in Detroit my mother and father owned a small family restaurant. When I was 10 years old they put me in the kitchen and started me washing pots and pans. The chef who worked there was really nice. He saw that I was very unhappy about this, so he thought he would show me a few things. So, I started making simple salads and sandwiches, and I really got into it. He noticed that I had a certain aptitude, so he started giving me more and more responsibility, until finally I took over his job at the age of 17. (He was ready to retire.) After high school I went to the Culinary Institute of America in New York City."

"Be assured that the Cilantro Champagne Cream tastes delicious with the lobster. Don't count your calories when you eat this.....it's a great way to splurge!"

Brett House

Frozen Lemon Ribbon Torte
with Vanilla Sauce

Frozen Lemon Ribbon Torte

1¾   cups fresh lemon juice
1⅓   cups sugar
6   whole eggs
2   egg yolks
¼   pound unsalted butter
3   drops yellow food coloring
1   9" round sponge cake
¼   cup Triple Sec
1   pint vanilla Häagen Daz ice cream, softened
       Vanilla Sauce *(recipe on next page)*
8   fresh strawberries, cleaned and quartered

In a small saucepan place the lemon juice and sugar, and bring them to a boil. Stir the ingredients until the sugar is dissolved. Set it aside.

In the top of a double boiler *(with the water simmering)* place the whole eggs and the egg yolks. Whisk them together.

While whisking constantly, gradually add the lemon mixture to the eggs. Whisk the mixture constantly for 5 to 7 minutes, or until it is smooth, thick, and creamy *(like a pudding)*.

Remove the lemon curd from the heat.

Add the butter and stir it until it has melted.

Add the yellow food coloring and stir it in.

Let the curd cool to room temperature.

Cut a ¼" thick slice off the bottom of the sponge cake. Place it in a 9" springform pan. Sprinkle on the Triple Sec.

Evenly spread on the ice cream so that it is ¼" thick. Freeze the torte for at least 30 minutes, or until the ice cream is hard.

Evenly spread on the lemon curd so that it is ¼" thick. Freeze the torte for at least 30 minutes.

Repeat the process with 2 more alternating layers of the ice cream and lemon curd.

Serve the torte with the Vanilla Sauce and garnish it with the strawberries.

serves 8

"This is a nice way to end a delicious dinner. The tartness of the lemon and the richness of the ice cream make a delightful combination. It's a refreshing dessert and it looks very pretty."

"Be sure that you use fresh lemon juice, and not bottled, which will give it a totally different flavor."

"Remember that when you add the hot liquid to the cold egg yolks you have to go very slowly in the beginning so that you don't scramble the eggs. Then towards the end you can go faster. Make sure that you keep stirring it in the top of the double boiler."

Brett House

Vanilla Sauce

1	cup heavy cream
¼	cup sugar
3	egg yolks
1	teaspoon vanilla

In a small saucepan place the heavy cream and sugar. Bring the mixture to a boil and stir it until the sugar is dissolved.

In the top half of a double boiler *(with the water simmering)* place the egg yolks and whisk them.

While whisking constantly, slowly add the heavy cream mixture to the egg yolks. Whisk the sauce for 5 to 7 minutes, or until it is slightly thickened *(a wooden spoon dipped in the sauce should come out lightly coated)*.

Add the vanilla and stir it in.

"The Vanilla Sauce is a simple, classic recipe that complements the torte really well. It's nice and smooth and rich."

"People call this dessert 'heaven'!"

"Another nice sauce that we serve with this torte is a raspberry sauce. Purée some raspberries with a little sugar and then strain them. The contrast of colors, with the red, yellow, and white, looks great!"

Window Detail, Ranchos de Taos, New Mexico

Carl's French Quarter

Modeled in the style of a fine New Orleans restaurant, Carl's French Quarter serves a mixture of continental and regional Creole cuisine. The decor is elegant, the atmosphere is relaxed, and the food is fantastic!

Menu

Carl's Light Vinaigrette
Carl's Margarita
Chicken and Piñon Nut Salad
Seafood Filé Gumbo
Shrimp and Artichoke Bisque
*Piñon and Chile
Pesto Fettucini*
Shrimp and Crab Thermidor
Chicken Picatta Milanese
Key Lime Pie
*Sacher Torte
Chocolate Brandy Glaze*
French Quarter Nudge

Owner Carl Fritz says, *"This dressing is very light, and it tastes so good that people don't realize they are eating something healthy!"*

Carl's Light Vinaigrette

½   cup red wine vinegar
2   tablespoons Dijon mustard
1   tablespoon orange marmalade
1   tablespoon parsley, chopped
1   teaspoon salt
1   teaspoon white pepper
½   cup light olive oil
½   cup light vegetable oil

In a medium bowl place the vinegar, mustard, orange marmalade, parsley, salt, and white pepper. Blend the ingredients together with an electric mixer on medium speed for 5 minutes.

With the mixer still running, add the olive oil and vegetable oil in a slow, steady stream. Continue mixing the dressing for 5 minutes more.

Carl's Margarita

½   cup lime juice, freshly squeezed
½   cup Cointreau
½   cup Grand Marnier
1   cup Herradura Gold Tequila
4   lime wedges

Fill a large pitcher with ice.

Add the lime juice, Cointreau, Grand Marnier, and tequila.

Stir the liquid until it is very cold *(the pitcher should sweat)*.

Pour the liquid into salted Margarita glasses.

Garnish each Margarita with a lime wedge.

serves 4

"A lot of people have their own secret Margarita recipe, but this one is the best I have ever found. People will drive up all the way from Santa Fe just to have one, and this is the truth!"

"The secret is to use the Cointreau and Grand Marnier instead of Triple Sec, and this allows the flavor of the tequila to come forward. So, it is important that you use a really fine tequila."

"Take the time to get the liquid in the pitcher very, very cold, so that the pitcher sweats."

"This is a tequila lover's Margarita!"

Chicken and Piñon Nut Salad

6	**cups vegetable oil** *(or as needed)*
4	**large flour tortillas**
½	**cup olive oil**
4	**chicken breasts, skin removed, boned, and diced**
½	**cup snow peas**
½	**cup carrots, julienned**
½	**cup yellow squash, julienned**
½	**cup zucchini, julienned**
½	**cup red bell peppers, julienned**
½	**cup mushrooms, sliced**
½	**cup scallions, chopped**
1	**small bunch cilantro, chopped**
½	**cup piñon nuts** *(or pine nuts)*
¼	**cup cooking sherry**
1	**cup lime juice, freshly squeezed**
4	**cups tossed salad greens**
1	**lime, sliced**
4	**sprigs cilantro**

In a deep fryer or a heavy pan place the vegetable oil and heat it on high until it reaches 375°. One at a time, place a tortilla in the oil and push it to the bottom of the pan with a ladle so that it forms a bowl shape. Hold the tortilla there until it is lightly brown and crisp. Remove the tortilla and drain it on paper towels. Repeat the process for the remaining 3 tortillas.

In a large skillet place the olive oil and heat it on medium high until it is hot. Add the chicken, snow peas, carrots, yellow squash, zucchini, bell peppers, mushrooms, and scallions. Sauté the vegetables for 3 to 5 minutes, or until they are slightly tender and hot through the center.

Add the cilantro and piñon nuts, and toss the mixture.

Add the sherry and lime juice. Toss everything together well. Remove the skillet from the heat.

On four individual serving plates arrange the salad greens. Place a tortilla shell in the center. Fill the shells with the chicken and vegetable stir-fry. Garnish the salad with the lime slices and the sprigs of cilantro.

serves 4

"This dish has a lot of different flavors in it, so you don't get hit with just one thing. First, there's one taste, like the chicken, and then the cilantro will hit another part of your mouth, and then you catch the taste of the piñon nuts somewhere else.....it's never a boring dish!"

"This is what I would eat in the summer as a meal, instead of a heavy dish. It's nice and light, and it tastes wonderful."

"One reason why I love Southwestern and Louisiana cuisines is that I like food that dances around in your mouth!"

Seafood Filé Gumbo

¼	pound butter
1	green bell pepper, chopped medium
1	medium yellow onion, chopped medium
2	stalks celery, chopped medium
2	tablespoons gumbo filé powder
½	teaspoon cayenne pepper
1	tablespoon paprika
½	teaspoon salt
½	teaspoon white pepper
½	teaspoon black pepper
½	teaspoon thyme
½	teaspoon oregano
1	bay leaf, crushed
1	tablespoon tabasco
1	tablespoon garlic, minced
1¼	cups chile sauce
4	cups chicken stock
¼	cup white rice, uncooked
1	tablespoon oil
4	ounces chicken meat, diced
4	ounces Andouille sausage, sliced
4	ounces ham, diced
3	tablespoons cooking sherry
8	ounces small bay shrimp
4	ounces fresh crab meat
1	cup okra, chopped

In a large, heavy pot place the butter and heat it on medium until it has melted. Add the bell peppers, onions, and celery. Sauté the vegetables for 3 to 4 minutes, or until they are barely tender.

Add the gumbo filé, cayenne pepper, paprika, salt, white pepper, black pepper, thyme, oregano, crushed bay leaf, tabasco, and garlic. Stir everything together well.

Add the chile sauce, chicken stock, and rice. Bring the liquid to a boil, and then reduce it to a simmer.

(continued on next page)

"There are as many gumbos as there are spaghetti sauces. My notion of a really fine seafood gumbo is this recipe."

"The okra and the filé powder are part of what thickens the gumbo. The Indians who lived in Louisiana were the Choctaws, and they discovered that sassafras leaves ground up, which is the filé powder, would actually thicken and season food."

"This is wonderful tasting, and it's very filling. Put a big pot of this gumbo in the center of your table, along with some good French bread, and you can call it a real winter meal."

"The ham, sausage, and chicken are the main background flavors to whatever seafood you are featuring in the gumbo. Use whatever kind of fish you can get that is fresh and good that day."

"The Andouille is a spicy Louisiana sausage. You can also use Kielbasa sausage, which is a smoked Polish sausage seasoned with garlic."

"Heinz makes a good chile sauce. It's sold in a bottle that looks similar to a catsup bottle."

"You can use crawfish tails instead of shrimp, and they taste great!"

"I have never had anyone who did not love this soup, it is so delicious. In fact, a number of people are addicted to it, and they will repeatedly come in to the restaurant and buy quarts of it."

"Remember that this recipe comes from the old school of cuisine where no attention at all was paid to one's health. It is very rich, and there is no question that you should not eat this soup every day of your life, even though you may want to once you taste it!"

In a large skillet place the oil and heat it on medium until it is hot. Add the chicken, sausage, and ham. Sauté them for 1 to 2 minutes, or until they are cooked through.

Add the sherry to the skillet and deglaze the pan. Add the cooked meats and liquid to the gumbo.

Add the shrimp, crab, and okra. Simmer the gumbo for 1 hour.

serves 4-6

Shrimp and Artichoke Bisque

¼	pound butter
1	medium yellow onion, minced
¼	cup flour
1	quart chicken stock
1	cup clam juice
2	cups half and half
1	cup heavy cream
1	teaspoon Worcestershire sauce
2	tablespoons tabasco
¼	cup pimientos, diced
1	tablespoon paprika
1	10-ounce can artichoke hearts
¼	pound bay shrimp

In a large stock pot place the butter and heat it on medium high until it has melted. Add the onions and sauté them for 4 to 5 minutes, or until they are lightly browned.

Add the flour and whisk it in.

Add the chicken stock and clam juice. Whisk the mixture for 2 to 3 minutes, or until it is smooth.

Add the half and half and stir it in. Add the heavy cream and stir it in. Bring the bisque to a boil.

Add the remaining ingredients and then reduce the heat to low. Simmer the bisque for ½ hour.

serves 4-6

Piñon and Chile Pesto Fettucini

4	ounces fresh basil
1	tablespoon garlic, minced
¼	cup piñon nuts *(or pine nuts)*
1	tablespoon olive oil
1	cup heavy cream
¼	cup mild green chile peppers, chopped
¼	cup Parmesan cheese, freshly grated
¾	pound fettucini, cooked al dente
½	cup Parmesan cheese, freshly grated
1	tablespoon piñon nuts *(or pine nuts)*

In a food processor place the basil, garlic, the ¼ cup of piñon nuts, and the olive oil. Purée the ingredients until they are well blended.

In a large skillet place the cream and heat it on medium until it starts to bubble.

Add the basil mixture, the green chile peppers, and the ¼ cup of Parmesan cheese to the cream. Stir everything together.

Add the fettucini and mix it thoroughly with the sauce.

Place the fettucini on a serving plate and sprinkle on the ½ cup of Parmesan cheese and the 1 tablespoon of piñon nuts.

serves 4

"The most common mistake people make when they are preparing pasta is that they don't use enough water when they boil it. So, you should use the biggest pot you have. The more water there is in relation to the pasta, the better the pasta will cook because the water won't be as starchy. When you bite the pasta it should be not quite cooked."

"The other mistake people make is that they don't wash it long enough. You should wash the pasta in cold water and toss it around with your hands. Do this for three or four minutes. Then set it in a colander and let it drain. If it sticks together then you haven't washed it long enough. So, if it is sticking together then you should wash it some more. Pasta is so much nicer and lighter tasting when it's washed well. That's the secret to making a good pasta."

"When you are ready to eat the pasta, then dip it into boiling water and drain it."

Shrimp and Crab Thermidor

*"The classic thermidor
that was around when I
was growing up was
made with lobster. But,
lobster is very expensive,
so I created this recipe
for people who wanted to
eat a luscious thermidor
at a reasonable price."*

½	cup clarified butter
8	large shrimp, peeled, deveined, and split in half
8	ounces bay shrimp
8	ounces fresh crab meat
½	cup cooking sherry
4	shallots, minced
1	cup mushrooms, sliced
1	tablespoon parsley, minced
1	tablespoon lobster base
1	cup heavy cream
2	tablespoons Parmesan cheese, freshly grated
1	tablespoon bread crumbs

*"It is possible to do this
dish with mock crab, and
it is so rich that it works.
It's not quite as good, but
it can be done."*

In a large skillet place the clarified butter and heat it on medium until it is hot. Add the large shrimp, bay shrimp, and crab meat. Sauté the shellfish for 3 to 5 minutes, or until the shrimp is barely done.

Add the sherry and deglaze the skillet.

Add the shallots, mushrooms, parsley, and lobster base. Toss everything together.

Add the cream and Parmesan cheese. Bring the mixture to a simmer.

Pour the mixture into a casserole dish. Sprinkle the bread crumbs on top.

Place the casserole under a preheated broiler for 1 to 2 minutes, or until the top is lightly brown. Serve it immediately.

serves 4

*"This tastes absolutely
scrumptious. When you
eat it you have that
sensuous feeling that you
are eating something that
is so rich and delicious,
that it's almost sinful!"*

Chicken Picatta Milanese

4	chicken breasts, skin and bones removed
1	cup bread crumbs, seasoned with salt and pepper
4	tablespoons clarified butter
½	cup white wine
¼	cup lemon juice, freshly squeezed
2	tablespoons capers
1	teaspoon garlic, minced

Cut each chicken breast into 4 equal pieces.

Pound the pieces between 2 sheets of waxed paper until they are thin.

Press the chicken fillets into the bread crumbs so that both sides are well coated.

Heat a large skillet until it is very hot.

Add the clarified butter. Add the coated chicken fillets and sauté them for 1 to 2 minutes on each side, or until they are golden brown.

Add the wine and lemon juice, and deglaze the pan.

Add the capers and garlic.

serves 4

"This is my personal, all time favorite, sentimental recipe of my life. And the reasons are that it is extremely simple to make, it can be done quickly, and people inevitably 'oooh' and 'ahhh' over it, as if you had done something really incredible! It is truly a wonderful recipe."

"Originally this was a recipe that was created for veal, and somehow in my past it was transposed to chicken, and it's great!"

"The better the wine, the better the flavor. If you happen to have a nice bottle of chardonnay that's open, then use some of that."

Key Lime Pie

1	**cup graham cracker crumbs**
¼	**cup powdered sugar**
½	**cup butter, melted**
4	**egg yolks**
½	**cup lime juice, freshly squeezed**
1	**cup sweetened condensed milk**
4	**egg whites**
1	**cup heavy cream**
1	**tablespoon powdered sugar**

In a medium bowl place the graham cracker crumbs and the ¼ cup of powdered sugar, and mix them together. Add the melted butter and stir it in.

Pat the mixture into an 8" pie tin to form a crust.

Preheat the oven to 350°. Bake the crust for 7 to 10 minutes, or until the edges turn golden brown.

In a medium bowl place the egg yolks and whisk them.

Add the lime juice and whisk it in.

Add the sweetened condensed milk and whisk it in.

In a small bowl place the egg whites and beat them until they are stiff, but not dry.

Fold the egg whites into the yolk mixture.

Pour the mixture into the pie shell.

Preheat the oven to 350°. Bake the pie for 15 to 20 minutes, or until the top is browned and raised.

In a medium bowl place the heavy cream and whip it. Add the 1 tablespoon powdered sugar when the cream is almost whipped.

Serve the whipped cream with the lime pie.

serves 4-6

"I think that any decent restaurant which serves a cuisine that is in any way connected to the deep South, absolutely must do a good lime pie. There are many different kinds of lime pie, and this is my favorite recipe. It works particularly well at our altitude, which is around seven thousand feet."

"The thing about key lime pie that is so attractive to people is the combination of sweet and sour. It's another dish that kind of dances in your mouth!"

"Be sure not to over-bake the pie. You need to experiment with your oven to learn exactly how long it should cook."

Sacher Torte
with Chocolate Brandy Glaze

Sacher Torte

10	ounces semi-sweet chocolate
1	cup butter, softened
½	cup sugar
12	egg yolks
1½	cups flour
12	egg whites
¼	cup raspberry preserves
	Chocolate Brandy Glaze *(recipe on next page)*

In a medium large saucepan place the chocolate and melt it.

In a medium bowl place the butter, sugar, and egg yolks. Cream the ingredients together until the mixture is very light.

Carefully fold the yolk mixture into the melted chocolate.

Carefully fold the flour into the chocolate mixture.

In a medium bowl place the egg whites and beat them until they are stiff, but not dry. Fold them into the chocolate mixture.

Pour the mixture into three 9" buttered and floured cake pans.

Preheat the oven to 325°. Bake the torte layers for 25 to 30 minutes, or until the tops look dry and the sides pull away from the pan. Remove the torte layers from the pan and cool them to room temperature.

On a serving plate invert one of the torte layers. Spread a thin layer of the raspberry preserves on top. Place a second torte layer on top, and spread on another thin layer of the raspberry preserves. Place the third torte layer on top.

Smoothly cover the torte with the Chocolate Brandy Glaze. Refrigerate the torte until the glaze hardens.

Add another coat of the Chocolate Brandy Glaze. Refrigerate the torte again until the glaze hardens.

serves 8

"This is an Austrian recipe and it's a real chocolate lover's dessert! The wonderful thing about it is the combination of the chocolate and raspberry flavors. This taste is the essence of the dessert."

"Dining out should be a total experience. It should be a pleasure to all of your senses, so that you want to say, 'THANKS! It's wonderful to be here!'"

Chocolate Brandy Glaze

6   ounces semi-sweet chocolate
½   cup butter, melted
1   tablespoon corn syrup
2   tablespoons brandy

In a small saucepan place the chocolate and melt it.

Add the butter, corn syrup, and brandy. Whisk the ingredients together so that they are well blended.

Strain the glaze through a fine sieve.

French Quarter Nudge

2   tablespoons heavy cream
1   teaspoon Frangelico
1   tablespoon brandy
1   tablespoon dark Creme de Cacao
1   tablespoon Frangelico
¾   cup hot coffee

In a blender place the heavy cream and the 1 teaspoon of Frangelico. Mix them together until the cream is slightly thickened.

In the bottom of a coffee cup place the brandy, the dark Creme de Cacao, and the 1 tablespoon of Frangelico.

Add the coffee.

Pour the flavored heavy cream on top of the coffee.

serves 1

"Cooking in a restaurant requires a certain skill in juggling. You need the ability to hold a number of things together in your mind, and then juggle them around in terms of the importance of their priorities. I really love it! It's a great feeling seeing everything coming together in the kitchen so that a beautiful plate goes out to the customer."

"This is the perfect drink to cap off a great meal.....and, to help you sleep! It's just a little nudge!"

"Put a little Frangelico into the cream. This is one of those simple little tricks that makes people ask 'WOW! How did you do that?' when they drink it. That's what changes an ordinary drink into something extra special. You know, like the alchemist turning lead into gold!"

Adobe Chimneys, Sagebrush Inn, Taos, New Mexico

Casa Cordova

Authentic Northern Italian dishes served with impeccable European style in an elegant old adobe home.....this is Casa Cordova! The excellent cuisine has earned this restaurant a national reputation for perfection in dining.

Owner Carlo Gislimberti, an expert in the collection and cooking of wild mushrooms, says that the translation of this recipe is "Mushrooms in Sauce".

"To make the croutons, slice a crusty loaf of bread, lightly brush the pieces with olive oil, and broil them until they are crispy on both sides. Spoon on the mushrooms, and eat them immediately, or else the croutons will get soggy."

Funghi in Umido

2	tablespoons oil
1	onion, chopped
½	clove garlic, finely chopped
1	cup Chantrelle mushrooms *(canned)*, **sliced**
1	cup fresh mushrooms, sliced
1	tablespoon fresh parsley, finely chopped
½	cup white wine
1	cup bouillon
2	tablespoons tomato sauce
	salt *(to taste)*
	pepper *(to taste)*
12	2" by 2" bread croutons

In a medium skillet place the oil and heat it on high until it is very hot. Add the onions, garlic, mushrooms, and parsley. Sauté the ingredients for 2 to 3 minutes, or until the mushrooms are seared.

Add the wine and reduce the heat to medium. Cover the pan and cook the ingredients until the wine has evaporated.

Add the bouillon and simmer the mixture for 20 minutes while stirring it occasionally.

Add the tomato sauce, salt, and pepper. Stir everything together.

Serve the mushrooms over the bread croutons.

serves 4

Stracciatella Soup

6   **eggs**
3   **tablespoons Parmesan cheese, freshly grated**
2   **teaspoons parsley, finely chopped**
1   **tablespoon bread crumbs**
1   **pinch nutmeg**
     black pepper, freshly ground *(to taste)*
6   **cups beef broth**
6   **cups chicken broth**

In a medium bowl place the eggs, Parmesan cheese, parsley, bread crumbs, nutmeg, and pepper. Whisk the ingredients together until they are well blended.

In a large saucepan place the beef broth and chicken broth, and bring them to a boil. While whisking constantly, very slowly add the egg mixture.

Let the soup boil for 2 minutes more without whisking it.

Remove the soup from the heat and serve it immediately.

serves 6

"I like this recipe because it is very easy to do, and it tastes delicious. It is something that I often make for myself, especially when I am tired after a hard day of work."

"The soup is very rich because of the eggs and Parmesan cheese. The trick is to have a very good broth. Have all of the ingredients ready to go before you start making it. Once the broth is boiling you add the other ingredients, and it's ready in three minutes!"

"Make sure that you use a good quality, fresh Parmesano, which will really increase the flavor of the soup. Don't buy pre-grated Parmesan!"

"This soup is a specialty of Rome and it is most popular in the summertime. And, of course, farm fresh eggs will do the trick, because the yolks will be much richer."

"This is a delicious dish from central Italy, where they have fresh veal. The word Saltimbocca means to 'jump in your mouth', so it's hard to translate into English!"

"The recipe is very easy to prepare, providing that the skillet is the appropriate size. You don't want to crowd the veal in the pan when you are sautéing it. Only in the end, when the veal is cooked in the sauce, can it be crowded."

"You can add a little bouillon to the sauce, if you have some, and that will make it better. Reduce the sauce to your desire. I am afraid to explain too much about the sauce because it would be too complicated!"

"I suggest serving this with a crisp, green salad, lightly dressed with olive oil and balsamic vinegar, and a little salt and pepper. Serve it with the veal, and not before. In Italy we serve the salad either with or after the main course, and not before it."

Saltimbocca Romana

8	**2-ounce veal scallops, pounded to ¼" thick**
8	**fresh sage leaves**
8	**thin slices prosciutto**
3	**tablespoons flour**
3	**tablespoons vegetable oil** *(or as needed)*
½	**cup dry white wine**
1	**tablespoon butter**
	salt *(to taste)*
	pepper *(to taste)*

In the center of each veal scallop place 1 sage leaf.

Place 1 slice of prosciutto on top of each veal scallop so that it covers the entire piece of veal.

With the back edge of a knife *(as opposed to the cutting edge),* lightly pound the prosciutto and veal in a checkerboard pattern, so that the prosciutto sticks to the veal.

Lightly dust both sides of the veal scallops with the flour. *(Be careful that the prosciutto does not fall off.)*

In a large skillet place half of the oil and heat it on medium until it is hot. Add 4 of the veal scallops and sauté them on each side for 2 minutes, or until they are golden brown. Remove the scallops and set them aside. Add the rest of the oil and repeat the process for the remaining 4 scallops.

Place the first 4 scallops back in the skillet.

With the heat still hot, add the wine and shake the pan. Let it flame. Keep shaking the pan for 1 to 2 minutes, or until the liquid is reduced by ½. Make certain that the veal scallops are evenly spread in the pan.

Add the butter and stir it until it has melted.

Place the veal scallops on a serving platter.

If needed, reduce the sauce further until it is creamy. Add the salt and pepper to taste.

Pour the sauce over the veal and serve it immediately.

serves 4

Polenta Cantandina with Gorgonzola

1	**cup milk**
7	**cups water**
1	**teaspoon salt**
1⅔	**cups polenta** *(or cornmeal)*
3	**tablespoons butter**
1	**tablespoon good olive oil**
1	**cup Parmesan cheese, freshly grated**
8	**ounces Gorgonzola cheese, sliced into 8 pieces**
	black pepper, freshly ground *(to taste)*

In a large saucepan place the milk and water, and bring them to a boil on medium heat.

Add the salt.

While whisking constantly, slowly add the polenta. Continue whisking until it is well incorporated and comes to a boil.

Cover the polenta with a lid and let it sit on the heat for 2 minutes, or until it thickens.

Remove the lid. Using a wooden spatula, stir the polenta in a clockwise motion every 2 minutes for 40 to 45 minutes, or until it is firm *(a crust will form on the edge of the pan)*. Lower the heat after 6 minutes. *(You may decrease the frequency of stirring as time goes on.)*

Prior to removing the polenta from the heat add the butter, olive oil, and Parmesan cheese. Stir them in.

Dip a ladle into cold water and scoop a serving of the polenta onto individual plates. Place a piece of the Gorgonzola cheese on top of each serving.

Grind on the black pepper.

serves 8

"Polenta used to be the bread of the poor people in Italy. Flour was not always available, and it was considered to be a luxury. So, polenta would substitute for bread."

"The best part of the polenta is the crust that forms on the edges, which is like nachos. You can eat it with cheese, and it's delicious! This is the secret treat that the chefs eat in the kitchen when they make this dish!"

"Originally, when I was young, I wanted to go to art school. But, due to circumstances I was not able to do that. So, I channeled my artistic urges into my cooking, using creative mixtures of tastes and textures, using lots of spices, and making good sauces."

"Zabaglione is a dessert that takes a very short time to make. Like the soup recipe, it also is very rich in eggs, so you shouldn't serve both dishes in the same meal."

"This dish comes from Sicily, where they make Marsala wine. It is a very ancient recipe that utilizes the local farm fresh eggs and the local wine. If you don't have Marsala, then you may substitute another sweet wine that you like. To serve it with the lady fingers is the classic Italian presentation."

"When you are whisking the mixture, the 45° angle rotary motion is very important. It incorporates air into the mixture. If you stop whisking for even one second, then it will be ruined, so be sure that you have a friend standing near you if you get weary of the stirring. This is a very tiring recipe!"

"In Italy they say this dessert will prepare you for the long, romantic evening ahead. The egg yolks are the secret of the young, Italian lovers!"

Zabaglione

4	egg yolks
¼	cup sugar
1	tablespoon white wine
1	tablespoon Marsala
6	lady fingers

Place a double boiler on high heat and bring the water to a boil. Do not let the top pan touch the boiling water.

Add the egg yolks and sugar to the top pan of the double boiler. Mix them together well with a wire whisk for 2 to 3 minutes, using a 45° angle rotary motion, until a creamy paste is formed.

While continuing to whisk, dribble in the white wine. Whisk the mixture until it lightens.

While continuing to whisk, dribble in the Marsala.

Continue to whisk the mixture for 1 or 2 minutes more, or until it is thick and foamy.

Spoon the mixture into attractive champagne glasses. Serve the dessert with a lady finger on the side.

serves 6

Cart Detail, Kit Carson House, Taos, New Mexico

Chile Connection

With a fireplace in every room, the Chile Connection offers delicious food served in a warm and friendly atmosphere. The festive decor, great drinks, and original New Mexican dishes put this restaurant at the top of the popularity list!

Menu

Chile con Queso and Chips

Judith's Green Chile

Hot Chicken Wings
Blue Cheese Dressing

Original Taos Salsa

Pueblo Beans

Nachos Supreme

Classic Guacamole

Taos Shrimp Twists
Hot Mustard Sauce

Pollo Borracho
Piñon Rice

Shrimp Chimichanga

Margarita Pie

Owner Richard Vick says, *"Buy the cheese sauce in the store, or else make a basic white sauce and add your favorite cheese. Heat the cheese sauce slowly.... don't burn it!"*

Chile con Queso and Chips

2 cups cheese sauce
1 tablespoon pimientos
2 tablespoons jalapeño peppers, seeded and sliced
1 tablespoon onions, minced
1 cup Judith's Green Chile *(recipe on next page)*
 tortilla chips

In a medium saucepan place the cheese sauce, pimientos, jalapeño peppers, onions, and Judith's Green Chile. Heat the ingredients on medium.

Stir the mixture until the sauce is hot and well blended.

Serve the sauce in a bowl with the tortilla chips on the side.

serves 4

Judith's Green Chile

2	tablespoons margarine
1	small onion, chopped
1	cup mild green chile peppers, chopped
2	tablespoons flour
½	teaspoon garlic powder
½	teaspoon salt
¼	teaspoon pepper
1	teaspoon vegetable oil *(or as needed)*
1	cup beef stock, hot

In a medium skillet place the margarine and heat it on medium until it has melted. Add the onions and sauté them for 2 to 3 minutes.

Add the green chile peppers and sauté them for 2 to 3 minutes.

In a small bowl place the flour, garlic powder, salt, and pepper. Mix the ingredients together.

Add the oil and mix it in. Add more oil, if needed, so that the mixture is not hard to stir, but not runny.

Add the flour mixture to the heated chile and stir it in for 2 to 3 minutes, or until the mixture is hot.

While stirring constantly, slowly add the hot beef stock. Bring the mixture to a boil and then reduce the heat. Simmer the sauce for 10 minutes. Stir it occasionally. Add more stock if necessary.

serves 4

"This is basically a thick chile gravy that we use as a smother on other dishes. If you add meat to it then you could call it a bowl of chile. Or, if you are a vegetarian, you could use a vegetable stock instead of a beef stock, and add beans to it."

"If you are using this as a smother, then it should not overwhelm the ingredients in the rest of your dish. It should just be an accent of flavor, and that is why we don't make it too spicy."

Hot Chicken Wings
with Blue Cheese Dressing

Hot Chicken Wings

1	**cup vegetable oil** *(or as needed)*
16	**chicken wings**
2	**sticks margarine, melted**
1	**cup catsup**
⅛	**cup tabasco**
1½	**teaspoons garlic, minced**
¼	**teaspoon white pepper**
	Blue Cheese Dressing *(recipe follows)*

"This is a great party dish. People love it and no one can tell what's in the sauce. They have no idea that catsup is one of the ingredients."

In a medium pan place the oil so that it is deep enough to cover one layer of the chicken wings. Heat the oil on medium high until it is very hot. Add some of the chicken wings and fry them for 4 to 5 minutes, or until they are crisp, but not dried out. Drain them on paper towels. Fry the remaining chicken wings in the same manner.

"The key to this recipe is that you should not be able to taste any of the individual ingredients in the sauce. So, if you can taste the catsup, then you need to add a little more garlic and tabasco."

In a medium saucepan place the margarine, catsup, tabasco, garlic, and white pepper. Stir the ingredients together. Heat the sauce on medium until it is hot.

Place the chicken wings in the sauce for 30 seconds.

Remove the wings and serve them with the Blue Cheese Dressing as a dip.

serves 4

"The level of hotness of the wings is determined more by how long the wings are in the sauce than by how hot the sauce is. So, don't worry if the sauce seems too hot."

Blue Cheese Dressing

½	**cup sour cream**
½	**cup blue cheese, crumbled**
1	**dash tabasco** *(or to taste)*
1	**dash white pepper** *(or to taste)*

In a small bowl place all of the ingredients and mix them together. Let the dressing sit for 5 minutes. Add more tabasco or white pepper if necessary.

"The Blue Cheese Dressing is fantastic with the Hot Chicken Wings. The tabasco and white pepper give it a subtle taste that makes it extra good!"

Original Taos Salsa

2	tablespoons margarine
1	small onion, diced
1	cup green chile peppers, chopped medium
½	teaspoon garlic powder
½	teaspoon salt
¼	teaspoon pepper
1	28-ounce can crushed tomatoes
¼	cup tomato juice *(or as needed)*

In a medium saucepan place the margarine and heat it on medium high until it has melted. Add the onions and sauté them for 2 to 3 minutes, or until they are translucent.

Add the green chile peppers and sauté them for 1 minute.

Add the garlic powder, salt, and pepper. Stir them in well.

Add the crushed tomatoes and stir them in.

While stirring constantly, gradually add the tomato juice until the desired consistency is achieved *(the salsa should be fairly thick)*.

Simmer the salsa for 30 minutes, or until the flavors are well blended.

"Our salsa is very thick and it stands up on the chip. The flavor and body come from the green chiles. Other salsas usually are made with chopped tomatoes and a little bit of jalapeño, and the consistency is thinner."

"I have tasted a lot of salsas that I didn't like, so I invented this one as something that I did like. I think it's outstanding!"

"One time a guy bought a gallon of this salsa. After he paid for it he said, 'Do you know what I'm going to do with this? I'm going to give it to a chemist and have him analyze it so that I can find out what the ingredients are.' So, I said, 'Gee, why didn't you just ask me? I gladly would have told you.' He didn't believe me, and just left!"

"This recipe came from a guy who ate in our restaurant many years ago. He came back to the kitchen and told me, 'I really love your food. The only thing that needs help is your beans.' It turned out that this guy had just won the world's bean cook-off! He gave me a couple of hints so that I could make a simplified version of his prize-winning recipe (which he didn't give to me). The two key ingredients are the bay leaves and the margarine."

"In our restaurant we go through every single bean before we cook them, to remove the little pieces of stone and debris that are there. People who see us picking through the beans have no idea what we are doing, so I tell them that we keep a really tight inventory in the restaurant, and we are just counting our beans!"

"I have to keep a sharp eye on the people in our kitchen to make sure they put in the bay leaves. They hate to pick them out, so they won't put them in if they think they can get away with it!"

Pueblo Beans

1	**pound pinto beans, sorted through and rinsed**
4	**quarts water** *(or as needed)*
1	**stick margarine**
5	**bay leaves**
1	**cup onions, chopped**
1	**tablespoon cumin**
1	**teaspoon garlic powder**
1	**teaspoon salt**
½	**teaspoon pepper**

In a large saucepan place the beans, water, margarine, and bay leaves. Bring the water to a boil and then reduce the heat. Simmer the beans for 4 hours, or until they are done. Add more water if necessary.

Strain the beans and reserve the water. Remove the bay leaves.

Add the onions, cumin, garlic powder, salt, and pepper to the beans. Stir the ingredients together.

Place the beans in a blender and purée them. Add the reserved water as necessary so that the beans are the consistency of mashed potatoes.

serves 10

Nachos Supreme

½   **cup vegetable oil**
8   **corn tortillas, quartered**
1   **cup Pueblo Beans, heated** *(recipe on previous page)*
1   **cup Original Taos Salsa** *(see page 56)*
1   **cup cheddar cheese, grated**
1   **cup Monterey Jack cheese, grated**
½   **cup sour cream**
½   **cup Classic Guacamole** *(recipe on next page)*

In a large skillet place the oil and heat it on high until it is hot. Quickly fry the tortilla pieces so that they are crisp. Drain them on paper towels.

Spread the Pueblo Beans evenly on the tortilla chips.

Place the chips on a large platter. Spoon some Original Taos Salsa on each chip.

Sprinkle on the two cheeses.

Place the chips in a preheated broiler to melt the cheese.

Place small dollops of sour cream and Classic Guacamole on each chip.

serves 4

"What makes these nachos special is that we take the time to put the different ingredients on every single chip. If you want to make lazy nachos, then you can just throw the stuff on top. But, if you take the time to address each chip, then every chip will be excellent!"

"Be careful when you spread on the beans. You don't want to break the chips."

"These are Cadillac nachos!"

Classic Guacamole

2 **large ripe California avocados, halved and pitted**
1 **small tomato, finely chopped**
1 **tablespoon onion, minced**
2 **dashes garlic powder**
 salt *(to taste)*
 pepper *(to taste)*

Dig the avocado meat out with a spoon and place it in a small bowl.

Add the remainder of the ingredients and blend them with an electric mixer until the guacamole is smooth.

"A lot of people will make guacamole with sour cream as a filler, because avocados are so expensive. So, I guess you could call this a rich man's guacamole because it's all avocado."

Taos Shrimp Twists
with Hot Mustard Sauce

Taos Shrimp Twists

1	pound cream cheese, softened
1	tablespoon pimientos, finely chopped
1	teaspoon vanilla
6	ounces bay shrimp, cooked
1	dash Worcestershire sauce
1	teaspoon lemon juice, freshly squeezed
2	tablespoons dried chives
16	egg roll wrappers
2	eggs, beaten
2	cups vegetable oil
	Hot Mustard Sauce (recipe follows)

In a medium bowl place the cream cheese, pimientos, vanilla, shrimp, Worcestershire sauce, lemon juice, and chives. Mix the ingredients together with an electric mixer until they are well blended.

Dip one side of an egg roll wrapper into the beaten eggs so that it is well coated.

Spread 1 tablespoon of the cream cheese mixture diagonally across the egg roll wrapper, 1" from each end. Fold it in half. Tuck the ends over. Roll it up and twist it. Do this for the remainder of the egg roll wrappers.

In a medium saucepan place the oil and heat it on medium high until it is hot. Deep-fry the twists for 1 minute, or until they are golden brown. Serve the twists with the Hot Mustard Sauce.

serves 4

Hot Mustard Sauce

¼	cup mayonnaise
½	teaspoon dry mustard
¼	cup water

In a small bowl place the ingredients and mix them together well. Refrigerate the sauce until it is chilled.

"This recipe was created by my beautiful new wife, Judith. She used all of the ingredients that she loves."

"The biggest trick is to have the ends of the egg roll wrappers tucked in when you roll them up. Also, be sure to use plenty of egg so that it sticks together. Otherwise, when you deep-fry the twist all of the filling will come out, and you will end up with a hollow egg roll!"

"These taste wonderful! They are meant to be an appetizer, but a lot of people will order them as a meal."

"Dry mustard can really vary in hotness, so you should be careful in making this. Start out small and then increase the amount to your desired taste."

Pollo Borracho
with Piñon Rice

Pollo Borracho

1	**tablespoon vegetable oil**
4	**chicken thighs**
4	**chicken drumsticks**
1	**cup rosé wine**
	salt (to taste)
	pepper (to taste)
	paprika (to taste)
1	**tablespoon butter**
½	**cup ham, diced**
½	**cup raisins**
½	**cup capers**
½	**cup green olives stuffed with pimientos, sliced**
	Piñon Rice (recipe follows)

In a large skillet place the oil and heat it on medium high until it is hot. Add the chicken pieces and quickly fry them on all sides until they are browned.

In a medium baking pan place the chicken. Add the wine. Sprinkle on the salt, pepper, and paprika. Place a dab of butter on each piece of chicken. Cover the pan.

Preheat the oven to 350°. Bake the chicken for 45 minutes.

Sprinkle on the ham, raisins, capers, and green olives. Cover the pan again and bake the chicken for another 15 minutes.

Serve the chicken with the Piñon Rice. Spoon the remaining liquid over the chicken and rice.

serves 4

Piñon Rice

3	**cups cooked white rice**
½	**cup piñon nuts** (or pine nuts)
1	**tablespoon dried parsley**

Mix the ingredients together and serve immediately.

"Clint Eastwood was filming his movie, Every Which Way But Loose. They were shooting some scenes in our restaurant, which they had leased for one day. The day before they were scheduled to arrive I got a phone call from the production company and was told that someone had put sugar in the gas tank of their caterer. By union contract they were obligated to serve a hot lunch, so they asked if I could cook a hot meal for a cast and crew of 130 people. I said okay, and, based upon what I had in my restaurant at the time, I came up with this recipe. Everyone loved it! Beverly D'Angelo came back to the kitchen to see how we made it. We were lucky it came out so good. The flavor is excellent, the ingredients are simple, and it's easy to make."

"When people ask for this rice recipe and I give it to them, they say, 'Oh, baloney!' They don't believe me because it tastes so good and it's so easy. But I promise you, it's true!"

Shrimp Chimichanga

4	flour tortillas, warmed to room temperature
2	whole mild, canned green chile peppers, cut in half lengthwise
24	small shrimp, shelled and cooked
1	tablespoon onions, finely chopped
½	cup Monterey Jack cheese, grated
½	cup cheddar cheese, grated
2	cups vegetable oil (or as needed)
½	cup Original Taos Salsa (see page 56)
½	cup cheddar cheese, grated
4	tablespoons Classic Guacamole (see page 59)
4	tablespoons sour cream
1	cup iceberg lettuce, chopped
1	cup tomatoes, chopped

Lay one tortilla flat. Place 1 green chile pepper half in the center. Place 6 shrimp on top.

In a small bowl mix the Monterey Jack cheese and the first ½ cup of cheddar cheese together.

Sprinkle ¼ of the onions and ¼ of the two cheeses on each tortilla.

Fold the 2 sides of the tortilla over the ingredients. Fold the ends over so that a square is formed and the tortilla is well sealed. Secure the tortilla with a toothpick. Repeat the process for the remaining 3 tortillas.

In a medium saucepan place the oil so that it is 4" deep. Heat the oil on medium high until it is very hot.

One at a time, place a stuffed tortilla in the hot oil and deep-fry it for 2 to 3 minutes on each side, or until it is crisp and lightly browned. Remove it with a slotted spoon. Poke a hole in the bottom of the smooth side to let any oil drain out.

Place the chimichangas on individual serving plates. Spread the Original Taos Salsa on top. Sprinkle on the other ½ cup of cheddar cheese.

Place the chimichangas in a preheated broiler so that the cheese melts.

Spoon on the Classic Guacamole and the sour cream. Serve the chimichanga with the lettuce and tomatoes on the side.

serves 4

"This particular recipe came into being because one customer kept bugging me about our not having any chimichangas on our menu. So, finally I gave in and said, 'Okay, but if I'm going to make a chimichanga then I might as well make it the way you like it, so tell me what you want in it!' So, he gave me his idea of what a good chimichanga was, and I took it from there. Now it's our top selling dish."

"My father is a mid-Western meat and potatoes man and he hates anything spicy. He won't even put any pepper on his food. But, he absolutely loves these chimichangas! He will eat the whole thing, and his plate will be so clean that you don't need to put it through the dishwasher!"

Margarita Pie

"The trick to this recipe is to beat the egg whites the correct amount. If they get too stiff, then the pie won't come out right."

"We've had tons of requests for this pie. However, be forewarned that this really tastes like a Margarita, so if you don't like tequila, then don't make it!"

"I believe that recipes should remain simple. If you use too many ingredients, then you end up masking the flavors of the food that you are dealing with. This is especially true of Mexican cooking, which is so basic and staple in its ingredients. The criteria is to use the best ingredients that you can, and then let the flavors come forward by just slightly enhancing them."

1	14-ounce can sweetened condensed milk
2	egg yolks
⅓	cup sugar
¼	cup lime juice, freshly squeezed
1½	ounces José Cuervo Gold Tequila
¾	ounce Cointreau
2	egg whites
1	9" graham cracker crust
½	cup heavy cream, whipped
1	lime, thinly sliced

In a medium bowl place the sweetened condensed milk, the egg yolks, sugar, lime juice, tequila, and Cointreau. Mix the ingredients together well.

In a small bowl place the egg whites and beat them until they are slightly stiff. Fold them into the egg yolk mixture.

Spoon the mixture into the graham cracker crust.

Preheat the oven to 350°. Bake the pie for 20 minutes, or until it is set.

Let the pie cool.

Refrigerate the pie for 1 hour, or until it is cold.

Serve the pie with the whipped cream and the lime slices.

serves 8

St. Francis de Asisi Church, Ranchos de Taos, New Mexico

Doc Martin's Restaurant

Located in the historic Taos Inn, Doc Martin's Restaurant has long been known for an innovative cuisine, a daily changing menu, and an award-winning wine list. All of this can be enjoyed in the several charming and intimate dining rooms.

Menu

Grilled Shitake Mushrooms
with Chipotle Dijonaise Sauce

Jicama Salad
Rice Wine Vinegar and
Sesame Ginger Dressing

Grilled Tuna with
Golden Tomato and English
Cucumber Relish

Salmon in Filo Pastry
Smoked Shellfish Mousse
Crayfish Sauce

Grilled Japanese Eggplant
with Red Onion and
Ginger Butter

Grilled Marinated
Pork Tenderloin
Roasted Corn and
Pasilla Chile Relish

Taos Dessert Tacos

Chocolate Capuccino Cake
Chocolate Glaze

Executive chef David Jones is the talented creator of these recipes. Having worked in France, New York, San Francisco, and Los Angeles, he brings a highly eclectic style to Doc Martin's.

Grilled Shitake Mushrooms with Chipotle Dijonaise Sauce

1   large egg yolk, room temperature
½   cup extra virgin olive oil
2   tablespoons white wine vinegar
1   tablespoon Dijon mustard
2   chipotle chiles, puréed
1-2 tablespoons sauvignon blanc
18 large fresh shitake mushrooms, washed and stems removed
1   tablespoon vegetable oil
½   cup Parmesan cheese, freshly grated
1   small bunch chives, finely chopped

In a small bowl place the egg yolk. Whip it with an electric mixer until it is thick and light in color.

With the mixer still running, very slowly dribble in some of the olive oil. When the mixture starts to thicken, add a few drops of the vinegar. Continue to alternate adding the oil and the vinegar, slowly, until the mixture is thick and well blended.

Add the Dijon mustard and puréed chipotles, and fold them in.

Add enough of the wine to make a thick, pourable sauce.

Lightly brush the mushrooms with the vegetable oil. Grill them for 4 to 5 minutes on each side, or until they begin to soften.

On 6 individual salad plates pour the sauce. Place 3 mushrooms on each plate. Sprinkle on the Parmesan cheese and chives.

serves 6

Jicama Salad
with Rice Wine Vinegar and
Sesame Ginger Dressing

Jicama Salad

2	cups jicama, julienned
¼	cup carrots, julienned
1	red bell pepper, julienned
½	bunch chives, cut into 1" pieces
1	cup Rice Wine Vinegar and Sesame Ginger Dressing
	(recipe on next page)
4	large leaves radicchio
8	leaves Belgian endive
2	small avocados, peeled and thinly sliced
1	lemon, peeled and thinly sliced

In a medium bowl place the jicama, carrots, red bell peppers, chives, and the Rice Wine Vinegar and Sesame Ginger Dressing. Toss everything together well.

Marinate the ingredients for 1 hour at room temperature.

On individual salad plates place the radicchio and Belgian endive. Place the jicama mixture on top.

Garnish the salad with the avocado and lemon slices.

serves 4

"Here is an example of a recipe with a combination of different influences. Jicama is a Southwestern root vegetable and I have combined it with an Oriental vinaigrette."

"This is a wonderful crispy, light, and non-fattening dish. It's very colorful and has a delicious fresh taste."

"If you would rather not have this as a salad, it also makes an excellent vegetable to serve with a meat or fish entrée."

"Through the years I have made a point of traveling to places all over the world where I am interested in the local cuisine. In my travels I've picked up the flavors and textures and smells of these particular cultures. I've brought them back to my native America, and then applied them to my profession."

"I think that dining should be a total experience of both sight and taste. I also like to think of it as somewhat playful and inventive!"

"This is a nice, light summer dish that is quick and easy to prepare. Use the best quality of olive oil that you can find. Make sure that the herbs are fresh.....and it's okay to substitute other kinds."

Rice Wine Vinegar and Sesame Ginger Dressing

¼ cup rice wine vinegar
1 tablespoon hot chile oil
½ teaspoon ginger, minced
½ teaspoon shallots, finely chopped
2 tablespoons tamari *(or soy sauce)*
2 tablespoons sesame seeds, toasted
½ cup sesame oil

In a medium bowl place the rice wine vinegar, hot chile oil, ginger, shallots, tamari, and sesame seeds. Mix everything together well. While whisking constantly, add the sesame oil in a very slow, steady stream.

Grilled Tuna with Golden Tomato and English Cucumber Relish

2 cups yellow pear tomatoes, cut in half
1 medium English cucumber, seeded and diced into ¾" cubes
2 bunches opal basil, finely chopped
¼ bunch fresh peppermint, finely chopped
3 tablespoons shallots, finely chopped
1 bunch chives, finely chopped
½ cup sherry wine vinegar
1½ cups extra virgin olive oil
salt *(to taste)*
pepper *(to taste)*
1 tablespoon vegetable oil
6 8-ounce tuna fillets

In a medium bowl place all of the ingredients except for the 1 tablespoon of vegetable oil and the tuna. Gently mix them together. Let the relish sit for 1 hour.

Lightly oil the tuna and grill it on both sides until it is just done. Spoon the relish on top.

serves 6

Salmon in Filo Pastry with Smoked Shellfish Mousse and Crayfish Sauce

Salmon in Filo Pastry

1	bunch leeks, washed
10	sheets filo dough
3	tablespoons clarified butter
4	4-ounce California King salmon fillets
2	cups Smoked Shellfish Mousse *(recipe on next page)*
1	bunch leeks, washed
3	tablespoons vegetable oil
1	cup Crayfish Sauce *(see page 70)*
½	pound mixed, smoked shellfish, shells removed
	(shrimp, scallops, mussels, crayfish, etc. – see chef's comments on this page for smoking directions)

Blanch the first bunch of the leeks in boiling water. Immediately place them in ice water. Cut the top part and bottom part of the leeks off, so that the remaining center part is 4 inches long. Slice the leeks in half, lengthwise, and set them aside.

For each serving lightly brush the clarified butter on 2 filo sheets and stack them on top of each other. Place ½ of another buttered filo sheet in the center. Place a few sliced leek pieces in the center. Place a salmon fillet on top. Place ½ cup of the Smoked Shellfish Mousse on top of the salmon.

Gather the pastry around the filling and tie it at the center with strips of leek. Repeat this process 4 times.

Preheat the oven to 325°. Place the wrapped salmon in a pan and bake them for 10 to 15 minutes, or until the pastry is golden brown.

Cut the top and the bottom parts of the second bunch of leeks off, so that the remaining center part is 4" long. Slice the leeks in half, lengthwise.

In a medium skillet place the oil and heat it on high until it is hot. Fry the leek pieces until they are crisp. Drain them on paper towels.

(continued on next page)

"This recipe was developed for a chef's competition. There is extensive preparation in this dish, although no one step is very difficult to do."

"Before you smoke the shellfish you should soak them in brine (one quart water, one half cup salt, and one quarter cup sugar) for a couple of hours."

"If you don't have a smoker then you must use a dome shaped charcoal grill. Light the charcoal and let it burn down awhile so that it isn't too hot. Then throw on some apple wood chips that have been soaked in water. Put the shellfish on the grill and cook them as slowly as you can, with as much smoke as possible. Don't overcook them!"

On individual serving plates pour some of the Crayfish Sauce. Place the wrapped salmon on top. Artfully arrange the mixed shellfish and fried leeks around the outside of the plate.

serves 4

Smoked Shellfish Mousse

1½   **pounds mixed shellfish, shelled, cleaned, and smoked** *(see chef's comments on page 68 for smoking directions)*
3   **large egg whites**
2   **cups heavy cream**
1   **tablespoon fresh thyme, chopped**
1   **tablespoon fresh chives, chopped**
1   **shallot, chopped**
¼   **cup sauvignon blanc**
2   **teaspoons white pepper**
¼   **teaspoon ground nutmeg**

In a food processor place the shellfish and purée it for 3 minutes.

With the food processor still running, add the egg whites.

Slowly add the cream.

Add the remainder of the ingredients and blend the mixture for 1 minute.

"The subtle flavor of the smoked shellfish is very nice, and the richness of the Crayfish Sauce really makes it an excellent dish. Visually, this is very striking!"

"The mousse can be prepared well in advance of using it. This is true for the other parts of the recipe as well."

Crayfish Sauce

3	**tablespoons olive oil**
1	**pound crayfish shells**
2	**tablespoons cognac**
2	**teaspoons clarified butter**
1	**pound carrots, chopped**
½	**bunch celery, chopped**
½	**bunch leeks, washed and chopped**
4	**shallots, chopped**
2	**tomatoes, chopped**
2	**cloves garlic, minced**
1	**bay leaf**
1	**clove**
3	**juniper berries, crushed**
1	**sprig tarragon**
1	**sprig thyme**
2	**tablespoons tomato paste**
	water *(as needed)*
1	**cup heavy cream**
1	**teaspoon salt** *(or to taste)*
½	**teaspoon black pepper** *(or to taste)*
½	**teaspoon cayenne pepper** *(or to taste)*
¼	**cup heavy cream, whipped**

In a large skillet place the oil and heat it on medium until it is hot. Add the crayfish shells and fry them for 5 minutes. Add the cognac. Remove the skillet from the heat and set it aside.

In another large skillet place the clarified butter and heat it on medium until it is hot. Add the carrots, celery, leeks, shallots, tomatoes, garlic, bay leaf, clove, juniper berries, tarragon, and thyme. Sauté the ingredients for 3 to 4 minutes.

Add the tomato paste and the fried crayfish shells. Stir everything together. Cover the ingredients with water and let them simmer for 45 minutes. Every 5 minutes remove any impurities that rise to the top.

Add the 1 cup of heavy cream and stir it in. Add the salt, black pepper, and cayenne pepper. Stir everything together.

Strain the sauce.

Slowly fold in the whipped cream.

"You can use shrimp if you can't find the crayfish. To get the shells you can use the ones from this recipe, and you also can freeze shells from other recipes that you have made in the past."

"I think that food should be visually appealing with a nice balance of colors. Also, I don't believe in crowding the plate with a lot of food, but then I don't believe in leaving the table hungry either! The correct proportions are very important."

"The Japanese eggplant has a richer flavor and is much more tender than the regular kind. The sweet red onion is a nice contrast to the grilled flavor of the eggplant, as are the ginger and vinegar."

"In California I worked with a lot of Oriental ingredients because they were readily available there. So, that was the inspiration for this recipe."

"American cuisine is difficult to describe because it is the combination of so many different influences, just as the American people are."

"I do extensive reading and research on cooking, and I eat out as often as I can in as many different types of restaurants as possible. So, I am influenced by lots of different chefs in this country. Also, I have been fortunate enough to have apprenticed under some really great chefs."

Grilled Japanese Eggplant with Red Onion and Ginger Butter

⅓   cup fresh ginger, finely chopped
¼   cup fresh shallots, finely chopped
3   tablespoons fresh garlic, finely chopped
1½   cups rice wine vinegar
½   pound unsalted butter, warmed to room temperature
1   small bunch chives, finely chopped
6   baby Japanese eggplants
1   large red onion, sliced into 6 portions
2   tablespoons vegetable oil
3   tablespoons scallions, finely chopped
3   tablespoons red bell peppers, finely chopped

In a small saucepan place the ginger, shallots, garlic, and vinegar. Heat the ingredients on medium and simmer them for 5 to 7 minutes, or until almost all of the liquid has evaporated. Chill the mixture in the refrigerator until it is cold.

In a medium bowl place the butter and whip it with an electric mixer until it is soft and light.

Add the chilled ginger mixture and the chives, and blend them in with the mixer.

Place the butter on a 12" by 12" piece of plastic wrap and roll it into a log. Chill the butter in the refrigerator until it is firm.

Start 1" down from the stem of each eggplant and make 4 slices lengthwise to the end of the eggplant.

Lightly brush the eggplants and onion slices with the oil. Grill them on all sides until they soften.

Place one onion slice on an individual salad plate. Fan out the eggplants and place one on top of each onion slice. Place a spoonful of the ginger butter on top. Sprinkle on the scallions and red bell peppers.

serves 6

Grilled Marinated Pork Tenderloin with Roasted Corn and Pasilla Chile Relish

Grilled Marinated Pork Tenderloin

½   cup sherry vinegar
1   cup olive oil
1   teaspoon garlic, chopped
1   teaspoon shallots, chopped
2   jalapeño peppers, seeded and chopped
½   teaspoon cumin
1   teaspoon salt
4   8-ounce pork tenderloins, fat trimmed off
     Roasted Corn and Pasilla Chile Relish *(recipe on next page)*

In a medium bowl place the sherry vinegar, olive oil, garlic, shallots, jalapeño peppers, cumin, and salt. Mix the ingredients together well.

Add the pork and let it marinate for 3 hours at room temperature.

Grill *(or broil)* the pork until it is just done.

Slice the pork into medallions.

On individual serving plates fan out the pork medallions.

Carefully spoon the Roasted Corn and Pasilla Chile Relish on the meat so that the medallions are ½ covered.

serves 4

"Pork tenderloin is very tender and flavorful. It can be grilled, broiled, or sautéed."

"This is a simple, delicious recipe that's perfect for a summertime outdoor barbecue. It's nice, light, and healthy!"

"Serve the dish with the Jicama Salad and some black beans."

"At first glance my cooking style might seem to be a little extravagant to some people. But when they try it they realize that it makes pretty good sense and seems to work. The ingredients might appear to be incongruous, but actually there is quite a bit of sophistication and classical background in their origins. I spent a long time mastering the classics before I began experimenting."

Doc Martin's Restaurant

Roasted Corn and Pasilla Chile Relish

"This relish has a lot of flavors of the Southwest in it, with the corn, cilantro, and Pasilla chiles. You can substitute a poblano chile or even a green Anaheim chile. The relish tastes great with the grilled pork!"

1	teaspoon vegetable oil
1	red bell pepper
2	Pasilla chiles
2	ears corn, roasted
3	tablespoons shallots, finely chopped
3	tablespoons garlic, finely chopped
1	bunch cilantro, chopped
1½	cups olive oil
½	cup sherry vinegar
	salt *(to taste)*
	pepper *(to taste)*

Lightly brush the vegetable oil on the red bell pepper and the Pasilla chiles. Roast them over a gas flame until the skin is blackened. Peel the skin off.

Remove the seeds from the pepper and the chiles.

Chop the pepper and chiles into small cubes.

Cut the corn away from the husks.

In a medium bowl place the cubed peppers and chiles, corn, and the remainder of the ingredients. Mix everything together well.

"One of the things that I like to bring to the table with my cooking is a sense of excitement and experimentation. I like to mix and match different cooking styles and ingredients, and then come up with my own particular style."

Doc Martin's Restaurant

Taos Dessert Tacos

1	cup mangos, peeled, pitted, puréed, and strained
¼	cup unsalted butter
1½	tablespoons lime juice, freshly squeezed
⅓	cup sugar
2	eggs
2	egg yolks
1	tablespoon unsalted butter, warmed to room temperature
6	tablespoons sugar
¼	cup egg whites
2	tablespoons flour
1	cup pine nuts, coarsely ground
1	cup fresh berries
½	cup heavy cream, whipped

In a medium saucepan place the puréed mangos and the ¼ cup of unsalted butter. Heat the ingredients on medium until the butter has melted. Stir the mixture frequently.

Remove the pan from the heat. Add the lime juice and the ⅓ cup of sugar, and stir them in until the mixture is smooth.

In a medium bowl place the eggs and egg yolks, and whisk them together until they are well blended.

While whisking constantly, add the puréed mango mixture to the eggs.

Pour the mixture back into the saucepan and place it on medium heat. While stirring constantly, cook the mixture for 10 minutes, or until it thickens to the point that it will lightly cover a spoon.

Strain the curd into a bowl and let it cool to room temperature. Cover the bowl and place the curd in the refrigerator until it is well chilled.

In a medium bowl place the 1 tablespoon of butter and the 6 tablespoons of sugar. Beat them with an electric mixer until the butter is light and fluffy.

While beating constantly add the ¼ cup of egg whites in 3 doses. Beat them in until they are well incorporated. Scrape down the sides of the bowl with a spatula.

(continued on next page)

"This is a variation on a classic French dessert called a 'tuile', which is a crisp pastry made with nuts. Traditionally it is in the shape of a tulip. My pastry chef and I were looking for something that would emphasize the Southwest, so we decided to make the tuiles in the shape of a taco and to use pine nuts."

"These aren't hard to make, but there are a lot of steps in the process. You have to make the shells and the mango curd separately. After these two things are done then it's very simple."

"I really like this dessert. The pine nuts go well with the sweetness."

"There is nothing too delicate or crucial in this recipe. Any one can successfully make it."

"In my cooking I like to use French techniques with fresh, local ingredients. I first learned how to cook in France, where I was lucky enough to get a job, even though I knew nothing about cooking!"

Carefully fold in the flour. Fold in the pine nuts.

Refrigerate the batter for 30 minutes.

Preheat the oven to 325°.

On a well-greased cookie sheet drop heaping tablespoons of the batter. Dip a fork into water and spread the batter into 4" circles. Leave 4" between the circles.

Bake the tuiles for 10 minutes, or until the edges are brown and the centers are pale gold. Remove the tuiles, let them cool for 20 seconds, and then, working quickly, mold them around a broom handle or rolling pin so that they form the shape of a taco shell.

Place each tuile *(taco)* on an individual serving plate. Spoon the mango curd into the folded tuile. Artfully arrange the berries on top. Garnish each tuile *(taco)* with a dollop of whipped cream.

serves 6

Chocolate Capuccino Cake
with Chocolate Glaze

Chocolate Capuccino Cake

22	ounces dark sweet chocolate, cut into small pieces
3	ounces strong coffee
1	tablespoon Kahlua
1½	tablespoons coffee extract
1	tablespoon vanilla extract
1½	cups whipping cream
¾	cup sugar
9	eggs
1	tablespoon cinnamon
½	teaspoon nutmeg, freshly ground
	Chocolate Glaze *(recipe on next page)*
1	cup whipping cream
2	tablespoons Kahlua

In a double boiler place the chocolate, coffee, the 1 tablespoon of Kahlua, the coffee extract, and the vanilla extract. Heat the ingredients on low heat until the chocolate has melted. Stir the ingredients together.

In a medium bowl place the 1½ cups of whipping cream and the sugar. Beat them together until soft peaks are formed. Cover the whipped cream, and set it aside.

In another medium bowl place the eggs, cinnamon, and nutmeg. Beat the ingredients together with an electric mixer until they are well blended.

While beating constantly on medium speed, slowly add the chocolate mixture to the eggs. After all of the chocolate has been added turn the mixer on high and whip the mixture until it is smooth.

Turn the mixer on medium and add the whipped cream. Whip the mixture until it is smooth and uniform in color.

Preheat the oven to 350°. Pour the batter into a well-buttered 10" springform pan. Place the pan in a larger pan filled with water. Bake the cake for 1 hour, or until it has risen and a hard crust has formed. Let the cake cool.

(continued on next page)

"At first glance this might seem like a complicated recipe, but actually it is very easy to make. It's hard to ruin this cake. I've made it sometimes with the sequence of ingredients in the wrong order, and it still came out good. It's not like a soufflé, or something that you can ruin if the temperature, or whatever, is not exactly right."

"This cake is flourless, and it is very rich. Basically it is chocolate and cream, so it's definitely not a diet food. Sometimes I think that the delicious taste of a dessert is a direct ratio to how bad it is for you!"

"If I go out to eat and want a dessert I will always gravitate towards something chocolate. My recipes usually reflect what I personally love to eat!"

Gently remove the outer ring of the springform. Place a round piece of cake cardboard on top of the cake. Invert the cake onto it. Carefully remove the base of the springform. Let the cake cool until it is set.

Gently pour the Chocolate Glaze over the cake. Make certain that the sides are evenly coated.

Chill the cake until the glaze is set.

Whip the 1 cup of whipping cream. Add the 2 tablespoons of Kahlua and stir it in.

Serve the Kahlua cream on top of the cake.

serves 8 to 10

Chocolate Glaze

12   **ounces dark sweet chocolate, cut into small pieces**
¼   **cup unsalted butter, warmed to room temperature**
¼   **cup water**
1¼   **cups whipping cream**

In a double boiler place all of the ingredients. Simmer the water until the chocolate has melted.

Whisk the ingredients together until the glaze is smooth.

"You can make the Chocolate Glaze in advance and keep it chilled. Just reheat it in a simmering double boiler when you are ready to use it, and mix it again."

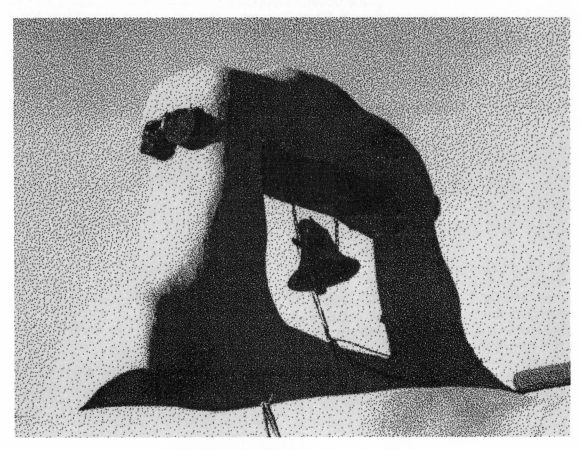

Adobe Belfry, Sagebrush Inn, Taos, New Mexico

Don Fernando's

Designed as an elegant, contemporary interpretation of ancient Pueblo architecture, the Holiday Inn Don Fernando's de Taos is a new premier resort hotel in Taos. Its attractive restaurant, Don Fernando's, serves a New Mexican cuisine that is both original and tasty.

Menu

New Mexican Cornbread

Tortilla Soup

Bad Hombre Eggs

Don Fernando's Green Chile Stew

Salsa Cruda

Don Fernando's Stuffed Peppers

Carne Adovada

Fernando's Red Chile Sauce

Gusdorf Chicken

Enchiladas Puerta Vallarta

Beef Fajitas

Taosino Club Sandwich

Dessert Tostadas

Food and Beverage Director Richard Bryant says, *"This cornbread is delicious! We did a lot of experimenting to get it just right."*

New Mexican Cornbread

2⅔   cups cornbread mix
2   cups water
¼   cup green bell peppers, diced
½   cup red bell peppers, diced
1⅔   cups Monterey Jack cheese, grated
⅓   cup creamed corn
¼   cup jalapeño peppers, seeded and diced
1   tablespoon honey
1   tablespoon red chile powder
1½   teaspoons sugar
½   teaspoon baking powder
1½   teaspoons flour

In a medium bowl place all of the ingredients and mix them together well.

Pour the batter into a greased baking pan.

Preheat the oven to 425°. Bake the bread for 25 minutes, or until it is done.

serves 8

Don Fernando's

Tortilla Soup

½	cup vegetable oil
6	corn tortillas, cut into wedges
1	tablespoon vegetable oil
½	cup green onions, sliced
2	teaspoons garlic, finely minced
3	cups cooked rice
1½	cups cooked chicken breast, skin removed, boned, and cubed
¾	cup green chile peppers, seeded and finely chopped
6	cups chicken broth
1½	tablespoons lime juice, freshly squeezed
1½	teaspoons salt
¼	teaspoon black pepper
¾	cup tomatoes, chopped
1	avocado, peeled, pitted, and diced
4	sprigs cilantro
1	lime, thinly sliced

In a large skillet place the ½ cup of oil and heat it on medium high until it is hot. Add the tortilla wedges and quickly fry them until they are crisp and lightly browned. Drain them on paper towels.

In a large saucepan place the 1 tablespoon of oil and heat it on medium until it is hot. Add the green onions and garlic, and sauté them for 2 to 3 minutes.

Add the cooked rice, chicken, green chile peppers, and chicken broth. Cover the pan and simmer the soup for 10 minutes.

Add the lime juice, salt, and pepper.

Pour the soup into individual serving bowls. Stand the tortilla wedges up around the side of each bowl. Sprinkle the tomatoes and avocados on top.

Garnish the soup with the cilantro sprigs and the lime slices.

serves 4

"This is our house soup and it's very popular. It's a spicy, tangy, chicken based soup with a lot of good things in it."

"The presentation of this soup is really fabulous. We place the tortilla chips all around the bowl and have them standing up. With the tomato and avocado pieces on top, and the lime and cilantro garnish, it looks really festive!"

"There are a lot of versions of tortilla soup, but this is one of the best I have ever tasted."

Don Fernando's

Bad Hombre Eggs

3	**cups vegetable oil**
4	**corn tortillas**
2	**tablespoons butter**
8	**eggs, beaten**
4	**tablespoons green bell peppers, chopped**
4	**tablespoons red bell peppers, chopped**
¼	**cup onions, chopped**
½	**cup tomatoes, chopped**
½	**cup Salsa Cruda** *(see page 83)*
2	**avocados, peeled, seeded, and diced**
¼	**cup cheddar cheese, grated**
¼	**cup sour cream**

In a medium saucepan place the oil and heat it on high until it is hot. One at a time place a tortilla in the oil and hold it down with a ladle to form a bowl. Drain the tortilla bowls on paper towels.

In a large skillet place the butter and heat it on medium until it has melted. Add the eggs, green bell peppers, and red bell peppers. Scramble the eggs together with the peppers.

In each tortilla bowl place ¼ of the scrambled eggs. In this order, top the eggs with the onions, tomatoes, Salsa Cruda, avocados, and cheddar cheese.

Place the filled tortilla bowls under a heated broiler to melt the cheese.

Place a dollop of sour cream on top of each serving.

serves 4

"'Bad Hombre' means 'bad man', which is just a catchy little title that we came up with to describe this delicious egg dish. It's very filling, and has a nice tang to it."

"The tortilla shell makes this dish really fun and festive, plus it tastes good to eat."

"If you don't want to make the tortilla shell then you can make this dish without it. Or, you can make a burrito by rolling the ingredients up in a flour tortilla."

Don Fernando's

Don Fernando's Green Chile Stew

½	pound ground chuck
½	pound ground pork
½	pound boneless sirloin, cubed
4	cups chicken broth
½	cup Mexican beer *(not dark)*
2	pounds poblano peppers, roasted, peeled, and chopped *(see chef's comments on page 119 for roasting instructions)*
1	tomato, chopped
2	tablespoons butter
1	medium onion, chopped
1	clove garlic, minced
½	cup fresh cilantro, chopped
2½	teaspoons tabasco
1½	teaspoons oregano
2½	teaspoons cumin
⅛	cup parsley, chopped
1	teaspoon salt
1	teaspoon black pepper
1½	tablespoons flour
2	tablespoons butter
1½	tablespoons flour

In a medium skillet place the ground chuck, ground pork, and cubed sirloin. Cook the meat until it is done. Remove the meat with a slotted spoon and place it in a large, heavy soup pot.

Add the chicken broth, beer, poblano peppers, and tomatoes. Bring the liquid to a boil and then reduce it to a simmer.

In another medium skillet place the first 2 tablespoons of butter and heat it on medium until it has melted. Add the onions, garlic, and cilantro. Sauté them for 3 to 5 minutes, or until the onions are softened.

Add the tabasco, oregano, cumin, parsley, salt, pepper, and the first 1½ tablespoons of flour. While stirring constantly, cook the ingredients for 3 minutes. Add the mixture to the soup pot and stir it in well.

(continued on next page)

"This stew has a unique and wonderful flavor. The cilantro adds a special taste to it."

"When I visited my home back in upstate New York I took some Southwestern ingredients with me. When I was there I prepared a big Northern New Mexican dinner for about twenty people, and this chile stew was one of the dishes that I served. It came out fantastic. It was a big hit with everyone!"

Bring the soup to a boil again and then reduce the heat to low. Simmer the soup for 2 hours. Stir it occasionally.

In a small bowl place the other 2 tablespoons of butter and the other 1½ tablespoons of flour. Knead them together.

While stirring constantly, add tiny bits of the butter and flour mixture to the soup. Simmer the soup for 15 minutes more.

serves 6

Salsa Cruda

2	**large tomatoes, peeled and chopped**
4	**tomatillos, husked and chopped**
2	**serrano chiles, seeded and finely chopped**
2	**jalapeño peppers, seeded and finely chopped**
5	**green onions, chopped**
1	**teaspoon lime juice, freshly squeezed**
1	**teaspoon fresh cilantro, minced**
1	**teaspoon cumin**
1	**teaspoon sugar**
¼	**teaspoon salt**
½	**teaspoon black pepper, freshly ground**

In a large bowl place all of the ingredients and mix them together well.

"This salsa has a unique taste because of the tomatillos and the serrano chiles. The tomatillos give it a little bit of a lemony, citrus flavor."

"The Salsa Cruda is heavy, crunchy, and great tasting. People go crazy over it. I really urge you to make it just once!"

Don Fernando's Stuffed Peppers

8	**Anaheim chile peppers, roasted and peeled** *(see chef's comments on page 119 for roasting instructions)*
1½	**cups Carne Adovada** *(recipe on next page)*
1	**cup Monterey Jack cheese, grated**
1	**cup bread crumbs**
1	**tablespoon chile powder**
1	**teaspoon cumin**
¼	**teaspoon salt**
⅛	**teaspoon pepper**
¼	**cup Parmesan cheese, freshly grated**
½	**cup flour**
4	**eggs, lightly beaten**
¼	**cup vegetable oil**

Slit open the peppers, lengthwise.

In a medium bowl place the Carne Adovada and the Monterey Jack cheese. Mix them together.

Stuff the chiles with the meat and cheese mixture.

In a small bowl place the bread crumbs, chile powder, cumin, salt, pepper, and Parmesan cheese. Mix the ingredients together.

Roll the stuffed chiles in the flour. Dip them into the beaten eggs. Roll them in the seasoned bread crumbs.

In a large skillet place the oil and heat it on medium high until it is hot. Add the breaded, stuffed chiles and sauté them for 5 to 6 minutes, or until they are golden brown on all sides.

serves 4

"This is a take-off on a chile relleno, but in an appetizer style. It's extremely popular, and there is no trick to preparing it. Once you have the Carne Adovada made (which you can do in advance), then it takes just minutes to make."

"Serve these peppers with a side of the Salsa Cruda, which I trust that you have made!"

Carne Adovada

12	ounces pork butt
2	cups water *(or as needed)*
1	teaspoon garlic, minced
1	teaspoon chile powder
½	teaspoon cumin
½	teaspoon salt
¼	teaspoon pepper
¾	cup Fernando's Red Chile Sauce *(recipe on next page)*

In a medium saucepan place the pork, water, garlic, chile powder, cumin, salt, and pepper.

Cover the pot and simmer the pork for 2 hours, or until it is so tender that the meat can easily be shredded with a fork.

Shred the pork and place it in a medium bowl. Add the Fernando's Red Chile Sauce and mix it together well.

makes 2½ cups

"You need to cook this for a long time, like a pot roast, so that it is super tender. It's very flavorful and spicy. You can use it in enchiladas, burritos, or whatever you want."

"My belief is that you see the food with your eyes before you taste it with your mouth. So, if the food looks really good, then your brain is already telling your mouth and stomach that it's going to taste great. Half the battle is already won!"

Fernando's Red Chile Sauce

8	large, dried New Mexico chile peppers
2	cups water
2	tablespoons jalapeño peppers, seeded and chopped
1	tablespoon jalapeño pepper juice
¾	teaspoon garlic powder
¾	teaspoon cumin
¾	teaspoon salt
2	teaspoons beef base
1	tablespoon oil
1	tablespoon flour

Preheat the oven to 350°. Place the dried New Mexico chile peppers in a pan and bake them for 10 minutes. Remove the stems and seeds.

In a medium saucepan place the water, dried New Mexico chile peppers, jalapeño peppers, and jalapeño pepper juice. Bring the liquid to a boil and then reduce the heat. Simmer the ingredients for 20 minutes.

Remove the chiles and place them in a blender. Pour in some of the water and purée the peppers. Add the rest of the water, the garlic powder, cumin, salt, and beef base. Blend the ingredients together well.

Strain the mixture and set it aside.

In a medium saucepan place the oil and heat it on medium until it is hot. Add the flour and stir it in. While stirring constantly, cook the roux on low heat for 3 to 4 minutes.

While continuing to stir, slowly add the strained, puréed chile mixture to the roux.

Bring the sauce to a boil and then simmer it for 5 minutes.

makes 2 cups

"The secret to the good flavor of this sauce lies in the baking of the dried chiles. So, even though this may be a little more work, it is really worth the effort. And really, it is not that much extra trouble. The chiles will be brittle at this point. They break apart very easily and the seeds fall right out."

"The sauce should be just thick enough so that when you ladle it on the item you are making, like an enchilada or chicken breast, it will adhere to it. You may have to adjust the amount of roux that you add to get the right consistency."

Don Fernando's

Gusdorf Chicken

"The Gusdorf Chicken is one of our most popular dishes. It's a nice, baked chicken breast prepared with a Southwestern flair."

"Instead of using the diced green chiles, you can buy the whole ones in a can. Slit them down the middle and cut them to the same size as the chicken breast."

"This is one of those great recipes that tastes wonderful, everyone loves, and is easy to make."

"The combination of the smoothness of the cheese and the crispiness of the crust is a wonderful contrast. And, the really neat thing about this recipe is that the chicken is baked, and not fried."

4	chicken breasts, skin and bones removed
4	tablespoons green chile peppers, diced
4	1-ounce strips Monterey Jack cheese
1	cup bread crumbs
¼	cup Parmesan cheese, freshly grated
1	tablespoon chile powder
1	teaspoon cumin
¼	teaspoon salt
⅛	teaspoon pepper
2	eggs, beaten
1	cup Fernando's Red Chile Sauce *(recipe on previous page)*
4	tablespoons sour cream
1	lime, cut into 4 wedges

Place the chicken breasts between 2 sheets of waxed paper and pound them until they are thin.

Spread one tablespoon of the green chile peppers on top of each breast. Place one cheese strip on top. Roll up the chicken breast.

In a small bowl place the bread crumbs, Parmesan cheese, chile powder, cumin, salt, and pepper. Mix the ingredients together well.

Dip the rolled chicken breasts in the beaten eggs.

Roll the chicken breasts in the seasoned bread crumbs so that they are well coated.

Preheat the oven to 375°. Place the chicken breasts on a flat sheet and bake them for 30 minutes, or until they are done and the coating is crisp.

Spoon on some of the Fernando's Red Chile Sauce. Place a dollop of sour cream on top. Garnish the dish with a lime wedge.

serves 4

Enchiladas Puerta Vallarta

3   **tablespoons butter**
8   **ounces crab meat**
8   **ounces bay shrimp**
¼   **cup vegetable oil**
8   **corn tortillas**
½   **cup Monterey Jack cheese, grated**
½   **cup green chile sauce, heated** *(see page 54)*
⅔   **cup Monterey Jack cheese, grated**
2   **cups green chile sauce, heated** *(see page 54)*

In a large skillet place the butter and heat it on medium until it has melted. Add the crab meat and shrimp, and sauté them for 3 to 4 minutes.

In a medium skillet place the oil and heat it on medium until it is hot. One at a time, briefly dip the tortillas in the hot oil so that they soften.

In the center of each tortilla place some of the shrimp and crab. Sprinkle on 2 tablespoons of the cheese. Ladle on 2 tablespoons of the green chile sauce.

Roll the tortillas up and place them in a baking pan.

Sprinkle the ⅔ cup of cheese on top. Place the enchiladas in a hot oven so that the cheese melts.

Ladle on the 2 cups of green chile sauce.

serves 4

"I believe that cooking should be fun! If you don't really enjoy cooking, or if you don't like what you are making, then the dish is not likely to come out as well. It's important that you personally like what you are cooking."

Don Fernando's

Beef Fajitas

1	pound sirloin, cut into thin strips
¼	cup soy sauce
¼	cup olive oil
⅛	cup red wine vinegar
2	cloves garlic, crushed
1	bay leaf
1	tablespoon orange juice, freshly squeezed
1	tablespoon lime juice, freshly squeezed
1	tablespoon lemon juice, freshly squeezed
⅛	teaspoon black pepper
⅛	teaspoon onion powder
1	green bell pepper, cut into thin strips
1	red bell pepper, cut into thin strips
1	yellow bell pepper, cut into thin strips
1	medium onion, sliced
½	lime
½	cup sour cream
½	cup guacamole
½	cup Salsa Cruda *(see page 83)*
1	cup lettuce, shredded
½	cup tomatoes, diced
½	cup Monterey Jack cheese, grated
8	flour tortillas, warmed

"The recipe for this marinade came from Abilene, Texas. It's great, and it can be used to marinate fish or chicken as well."

"When you squeeze the lime juice on top of the sizzling meat, a delicious aroma is emitted. The smell gets everyone's attention and mouths start watering."

"This dish makes a wonderful presentation. It's really fun to serve at a dinner party."

"You can put the different garnish items on each individual plate, or you can put them in small bowls, and let each person take whatever he or she wants."

In a medium glass or stainless steel bowl place the sirloin strips, soy sauce, olive oil, vinegar, garlic, bay leaf, orange juice, lime juice, lemon juice, pepper, and onion powder. Mix the ingredients together. Cover the bowl and place it in the refrigerator overnight.

Remove the sirloin strips with a slotted spoon.

Heat a cast iron skillet over high heat until it is extremely hot. Add the sirloin strips, bell peppers, and onions. Sauté the ingredients for 2 to 3 minutes.

Squeeze the juice of the ½ lime onto the mixture.

Place the fajitas on individual serving plates. Serve them with the sour cream, guacamole, Salsa Cruda, lettuce, tomatoes, cheese, and warm tortillas.

serves 4

Don Fernando's

Taosino Club Sandwich

4	large flour tortillas, warmed on both sides
½	cup guacamole
½	cup Monterey Jack cheese, grated
12	ounces cooked chicken breast, skinned, boned, and shredded
12	strips bacon, cooked
½	cup iceberg lettuce, shredded
12	slices tomato

On each of the tortillas spread the guacamole so that the tortilla is completely covered.

On one half of each tortilla place the cheese, chicken, 3 strips of the bacon, lettuce, and 3 slices of the tomato.

Roll the tortillas up and then cut them into 4 sections.

Stick a toothpick in each section. Stand the sections up on an individual serving plate.

serves 4

"This is a Southwestern version of the very popular club sandwich. You notice that we use guacamole instead of mayonnaise."

"We are under debate as to who is the creator of this recipe. One person said he made it up, and another said he used to make the same thing at another restaurant he had previously worked in. I guess it doesn't matter where the recipe came from.....what matters is that it tastes great!"

"We stand the sections of the rolled tortilla up on the plate so you can look down and see all the different swirls of color. They look really pretty."

Dessert Tostadas

3	cups vegetable oil
4	8" flour tortillas
4	egg yolks
¼	teaspoon vanilla extract
½	cup sugar
1½	cups heavy cream
½	teaspoon lemon juice
4	ounces bittersweet chocolate, melted
2	cups assorted fresh fruit, sliced
4	tablespoons dark brown sugar

In a medium saucepan place the oil and heat it on high until it is hot. One at a time, place a tortilla in the hot oil and hold it down with a ladle to form a crispy bowl. Drain the bowls on paper towels.

In a small bowl place the egg yolks and beat them until they are light and lemon colored.

Add the vanilla extract and sugar, and beat them in until the mixture is thick.

In another small bowl place the heavy cream and lemon juice, and mix them together.

Pour the egg mixture into the top of a simmering double boiler.

While beating constantly, add the heavy cream mixture. Beat the mixture until it thickens and will coat the back of a wooden spoon. *(Do not allow the mixture to boil.)*

Cover the custard with saran wrap and let it cool to room temperature. Place the custard in the refrigerator for 1 hour.

Paint the outside of the tortilla cups with the melted chocolate.

Place the fruit in the cups. Spoon the custard on top.

Sprinkle on the dark brown sugar.

Place the filled tortilla cups under the broiler so that the sugar caramelizes.

serves 4

"You can use any kind of fresh fruit that is in season. Strawberries are very nice because of their red color, which looks visually striking next to the light cream color of the custard."

"If you are feeling lazy, you can just make a packaged vanilla pudding instead of the custard."

Taos Pueblo, New Mexico

El Patio

If you want to experience a classic European cuisine that is served in the historic, oldest adobe building in Taos, then El Patio is it! The service is professional, the ambiance is pleasant, and the food is perfection.

Yvon Bahic, the French-born owner of El Patio, has had extensive experience in both Europe and America. He says, *"This is an Italian recipe. It has so many items in it that it's like a little meal."*

Escargot El Patio

½	cup clarified butter
24	escargot
2	teaspoons garlic, minced
½	cup mushrooms, sliced
1	teaspoon shallots, finely chopped
¼	cup white wine
1	medium tomato, diced
2	tablespoons walnuts, broken
2	teaspoons fresh parsley, chopped

In a medium sauté pan place the butter and heat it on high until it is hot.

Add the escargot, garlic, mushrooms, and shallots. Shake the pan and keep the ingredients moving for 5 minutes.

Add the wine and flambé it. Reduce the heat to low.

Add the tomatoes, walnuts, and parsley. Cook the ingredients for 2 minutes.

Serve the escargot in small individual bowls.

serves 4

Lettuce Soup

6	cups water
2	large potatoes, diced large
1	medium onion, diced large
3	chicken bouillon cubes
1	head iceberg lettuce, chopped
½	cup milk
1	teaspoon black pepper
2	teaspoons butter

In a medium large saucepan place the water, potatoes, onions, and chicken bouillon cubes. Bring the ingredients to a boil and cook them for 30 minutes, or until the potatoes crumble.

Add the lettuce, milk, and pepper. Boil the ingredients for 10 minutes.

Add the butter and stir it in.

Place the soup in a blender and purée it until it is smooth.

Reheat the soup when you are ready to serve it.

serves 4

"My grandmother used to make this soup in France. She would save the lettuce leaves that didn't look nice enough to put in a salad, and then she would make a soup out of them."

"This soup is very tasty! Its flavor is similar to that of watercress, only it's lighter. Iceberg lettuce is what you should use, because the flavor is best. Other kinds of lettuce may taste too strong or bitter."

Hot Spinach Salad with Cognac Dressing

1   **large egg yolk**
¼   **cup red wine vinegar**
1   **cup salad oil**
5   **tablespoons Dijon mustard**
1   **pinch salt** *(or to taste)*
1   **pinch pepper** *(or to taste)*
2   **bunches spinach, stems removed, washed and dried**
½   **cup olive oil**
1   **teaspoon cracked black pepper**
12   **strips bacon, fried and crumbled**
¼   **cup cognac**
¼   **cup white wine**

In a small bowl place the egg yolk and whip it.

Add the vinegar and mix it in.

Add the salad oil and mustard, and whip them in until the mixture is smooth.

Add the salt and pepper, and mix them in. Refrigerate the dressing for ½ hour.

In a large salad bowl place the spinach. Pour on the chilled dressing and toss it well.

In a medium sauté pan place the olive oil and heat it on high until it is hot. Add the cracked black pepper and bacon pieces, and sauté them for 30 seconds.

Add the cognac and flambé it.

Add the wine and flambé it.

Pour the hot mixture on the spinach and toss it so that all of the leaves are well coated.

Cover the spinach with a lid for 2 to 3 minutes, and then serve it immediately.

serves 4

"Try to get the best fresh spinach that you can. If you can pick it fresh from your garden, then all the better."

"This salad is very easy to make and it has a wonderful flavor. The purpose of covering the spinach after you pour the hot dressing on it is to steam the leaves so that they become warm and wilted. But don't steam them too long."

El Patio

Linguini alla Puttanesca

1   **cup half and half**
6   **tablespoons heavy cream**
1   **teaspoon cracked black pepper**
3   **teaspoons Parmesan cheese, freshly grated**
12   **anchovies, diced**
1   **medium tomato, diced**
2   **teaspoons capers**
½   **cup mushrooms, sliced**
8   **ounces fresh linguini, cooked al dente, rinsed, and held in a cold water bath**
¼   **cup Parmesan cheese, freshly grated**

In a large sauté pan place the half and half, heavy cream, black pepper, the 3 teaspoons of Parmesan cheese, the anchovies, tomatoes, capers, and mushrooms.

Slowly bring the ingredients to a boil. While stirring constantly, boil the mixture for 5 minutes.

Place the linguini in hot water for 1 minute and then drain it.

Add the linguini to the sauce and quickly stir it in.

Serve the linguini immediately. Sprinkle the ¼ cup of Parmesan cheese on top.

serves 4

"This is an Italian recipe that comes from the northern lake district, especially around Lake Como."

"The anchovies and capers are the two essential tastes, and they blend together very well. Try to get the best quality of anchovies possible."

"If you don't like anchovies you can use less than what the recipe calls for. Or, you can use more if you really love them."

"'Puttanesca' means 'the naughty woman in the street'!"

"This is a very delicious tasting dish. It's a classical recipe from France that you will find in many European restaurants. It's not rich.....it's very light."

"The fillets should be large, thin, and flat. The Dover sole is the best. You can make the mousse with salmon, which in a way is nicer, because the color of the red looks prettier. If you use the salmon, the recipe will be exactly the same as with the scallops, except that you will need to add a little more of the egg white, and some half and half, to thin it out."

"If you don't have a pastry bag, then use a spoon to put the mousse on the sole. And, when you wrap the sole in the parchment paper, be sure to tuck the ends in tightly so that they are well sealed. The flavor of the broth comes through the paper."

Fillet of Dover Sole with Scallop Mousse

8	ounces bay scallops
1	large egg white
1	tablespoon heavy cream
1	pinch white pepper
1	pinch granulated garlic
8	4-ounce fillets of Dover sole
½	cup butter, melted
1	quart water
3	fish bouillon cubes
1	tablespoon lemon juice, freshly squeezed

In a food processor place the scallops, egg white, heavy cream, white pepper, and garlic. Blend the ingredients together until the mixture is smooth. Place the mousse in a pastry bag.

Cut eight 4" by 6" pieces of parchment paper.

Lay 1 piece of the sole in the middle of 1 piece of the parchment paper.

Pipe out ¼ of the mousse from the pastry bag onto the center of the sole. Place a second piece of sole on top.

Lightly brush the butter on the paper around the sole.

Place a second piece of parchment paper on top of the sole and tuck it under. Roll the paper and fish up 1½ times. Tuck the ends in tightly.

In a medium saucepan place the water and fish bouillon cubes. Bring the water to a boil and dissolve the cubes.

Preheat the oven to 450°. In a shallow baking pan place the broth and the wrapped fish, and bake them for 10 minutes.

Remove the fish from the broth and carefully unwrap them.

Add the lemon juice to the remaining melted butter.

Coat the fish with the lemon butter.

serves 4

El Patio

Rack of Lamb
with Mint Sauce

Rack of Lamb

2   **center cut racks of lamb, halved**
3   **tablespoons olive oil**
2   **tablespoons dry oregano, crushed**
1   **tablespoon cracked black pepper**
3   **cloves garlic, crushed**
       Mint Sauce *(recipe on next page)*

Rub the racks of lamb with the oil, dry oregano, black pepper, and garlic.

In a large, hot skillet, quickly brown the racks.

Preheat the oven to 400°. In a large baking pan place the racks and bake them for 15 to 25 minutes *(15 minutes for rare, 20 minutes for medium, and 25 minutes for well done)*.

Pour the Mint Sauce over the racks.

serves 4

"This is another French recipe that I learned to make in Europe. It's very simple and straight-forward, and it will come out perfect every time. We serve it at the restaurant and it's very popular. People love it!"

"Our customers come back to eat here time and time again. They enjoy sitting in our dining room with the fountain. And, of course, they enjoy the food."

Mint Sauce

¼ **cup red wine**
1 **clove garlic, minced**
1 **teaspoon fresh oregano, chopped**
1 **tablespoon brown sugar**
1 **teaspoon red wine vinegar**
¼ **cup red wine**
½ **cup beef broth**
2 **tablespoons fresh mint, chopped**
1 **teaspoon tomato juice**
1 **tablespoon cornstarch**
1 **teaspoon cold water**

Heat a medium sauté pan until it is hot. Add the first ¼ cup of red wine, the garlic, oregano, brown sugar, and red wine vinegar.

While stirring constantly, cook the mixture until the sugar is caramelized.

Add the other ¼ cup of red wine, the beef broth, mint, and tomato juice. Simmer the sauce for 10 minutes.

Strain the sauce through a fine sieve.

In a small bowl place the cornstarch and cold water, and mix them together.

Place the strained broth in a small saucepan and heat it on medium. Add the cornstarch and stir it in. While stirring constantly, cook the sauce for 3 to 4 minutes.

"We don't use a mint jelly, which is a very common thing to serve with lamb. In this recipe we use fresh mint. This sauce is really excellent."

"All of my sauces are very light. They are just to complement the main ingredient. If I buy a lamb, then I want to prepare it in such a way that I can really taste the lamb, rather than tasting a lot of the other ingredients."

Roast Duck
with Grand Marnier Sauce

Roast Duck

2   5-pound ducks, whole
Grand Marnier Sauce *(recipe on next page)*

Preheat the oven to 400°. In a large baking pan place the ducks, breast side down. Roast them for 1½ hours.

Remove the ducks and drain off the grease. Let the ducks cool.

Split the ducks in half. Remove the rib bones.

Preheat the oven to 400°. Set a rack in a baking pan and place the de-boned ducks on top.

Bake the ducks for 15 minutes.

Spoon the Grand Marnier Sauce over the ducks.

serves 4

"You can tell when the duck is ready to be removed from the oven by sticking a knife into it. Leave it there and count to ten. Then put the knife to your lips. If it feels very hot then the duck is ready."

"It is easy to de-bone the duck, although it would be better if you could watch someone else do it first."

"At our restaurant we have a maître d' who welcomes the customers, seats them, puts the serviette on their laps, and explains the specials to them. He, as well as all of the people who work here, must be very knowledgeable about all of the sauces and different dishes that we serve. This is very difficult, because we always offer so many specials that change daily."

El Patio

Grand Marnier Sauce

½ **cup granulated sugar**
1 **teaspoon white vinegar**
3 **cups water**
2 **cubes chicken bouillon**
3 **tablespoons orange juice, freshly squeezed**
3 **tablespoons lemon juice, freshly squeezed**
3 **tablespoons tomato sauce**
¼ **cup Grand Marnier**

In a medium saucepan place the sugar and vinegar. While stirring constantly, heat the mixture on medium high until the sugar is caramelized.

In another medium saucepan place the water and chicken bouillon cubes. Bring the water to a boil and dissolve the cubes.

While stirring constantly, slowly add the hot bouillon to the caramelized sugar.

Add the orange juice, lemon juice, and tomato sauce. Stir the sauce and let it simmer for 20 minutes.

Add the Grand Marnier and flambé it.

"You can serve duck with many different sauces, but probably Duck à la Orange is the most popular. This particular recipe is the best I have found for an orange sauce."

"Make certain that the pan you make this sauce in is completely clean and that there is absolutely no grease in it. The same goes for the spoon. Otherwise the caramelized sugar will be ruined."

"If you want, you can save the bones from the duck, and then use them to make a stock for this recipe, instead of using the chicken bouillon cubes."

French Baguette

⅔ **cup cold water**
½ **teaspoon salt**
1⅛ **cups high gluten flour**
½ **tablespoon dry yeast**

In a medium bowl place all of the ingredients. With an electric mixer beat them together for 5 minutes on low speed.

Cover the bowl and place it in a warm spot in the kitchen. Let the dough sit for 1 hour.

Beat the dough down. Roll it into a ball. Place the dough back in the bowl, cover it, and let it sit for 40 minutes.

Flatten out the dough with a rolling pin. Fold it in half. Fold it in half again. Repeat this process 4 times.

Fold the dough again. Seal the seams together. Using your hands, roll out the dough to form a 24" long loaf. Place the loaf on a flat baking sheet.

Brush the top of the loaf with water. Cover the loaf with a damp towel. Let it rise until it has doubled in size.

Using a knife, make 4 slits in the top of the loaf at a 45° angle.

Preheat the oven to 400°. Bake the loaf for 30 minutes, or until it turns golden brown.

makes 1 loaf

"The secret to this recipe lies in the kneading of the dough. It is easier to make if you have a strong, electric mixer. You may want to divide the dough in half, and make two smaller loaves."

"The time that it will take the dough to rise depends upon how warm your kitchen is. Be sure that the dough doesn't dry out, and keep it out of drafts."

"You can brush the top of the loaf with flour, instead of water, before you bake it. This will give it a 'country' effect."

Crêpes Suzette

2	large eggs
½	cup flour
1	cup milk
¾	cup brown sugar
4	oranges, juiced
4	lemons, juiced
2	ounces cognac

In a medium bowl place the eggs. Beat them well with a wire whisk.

While whisking constantly, slowly add the flour.

When the wire whisk starts to clog up, add the milk. Whisk the batter until it is very smooth and loose.

Place a 7" teflon sauté pan on medium high heat. Place 2 tablespoons of the batter in the pan. Spread it around so that it covers the entire pan. Cook it until the sides peel away from the pan. Gently turn the crêpe over with a spatula. Cook the other side for ½ minute. Remove the crêpe from the pan and let it cool. Repeat this process until 12 crêpes are made.

In a medium large sauté pan place the brown sugar. While stirring constantly, heat the sugar on medium until it caramelizes.

Add the orange juice and the lemon juice, and mix them in.

Reduce the heat to low. One at a time, add the crêpes to the sauce and fold them twice, so that they are in a triangular shape. Remove the crêpes and place them on a platter.

Add the cognac to the sauce and flambé it. Pour the sauce over the crêpes.

serves 6

"Crêpes Suzette are very popular all over Europe. They also are served in many good restaurants in America, especially in big cities like New York and San Francisco."

"This is a classic French recipe, and it is very easy to make. Be sure that you make the crêpes as thin as possible. Many people make them too thick."

"You may use Grand Marnier to flambé the sauce, which gives you more of an orange taste. Or, you can use brandy. Also, you can put fruit inside the crêpes, such as peaches or strawberries."

"The lemon juice cuts the acidity of the orange juice. It seems strange that two acids will do this, but it's true!"

Horno Detail, Millicent Rogers Museum, Taos, New Mexico

Garden Restaurant

Warm, cozy, and friendly, the Garden Restaurant reminds one of an inviting family style Alpine chalet. The hearty food is simple but delicious, and it's a wonderful place to eat at any time of the day or night.

Owner Yvon Bahic (who also owns El Patio) grew up eating this soup as a small boy in France.

"This soup tastes better the second day, and even better the third!"

Lentil Soup

2   **tablespoons olive oil**
1   **onion, chopped**
1   **bunch scallions, chopped**
1   **carrot, chopped**
2   **cloves garlic, minced**
8   **cups chicken broth**
1   **cup dried lentils**
    salt *(to taste)*
    pepper *(to taste)*

In a large skillet place the olive oil and heat it on medium until it is hot. Add the onions, scallions, carrots, and garlic. Reduce the heat and slowly sauté the vegetables for 10 minutes. Drain the vegetables and set them aside.

In a large saucepan place the chicken broth and bring it to a boil.

Add the lentils and reduce the heat to low. Simmer the lentils for 1 hour.

Add the sautéed vegetables and simmer the soup for ½ hour more.

Add the salt and pepper.

serves 4-6

Taco Shell Salad
with Garden Dressing

Taco Shell Salad

4	cups vegetable oil
4	medium flour tortillas
1	head leaf lettuce, washed, dried, and torn
1	carrot, peeled and grated
1	cup alfalfa sprouts
1	small cucumber, peeled and sliced
1	cup mushrooms, thinly sliced
½	cup ham, diced
½	cup Swiss cheese, diced
1	avocado, peeled, pitted, and sliced
1	hard-boiled egg, peeled and sliced
1	tomato, cut into 8 wedges
8	black olives, pitted and cut in half
	Garden Dressing *(recipe on next page)*

In a medium saucepan place the oil and heat it on medium high until it is hot. Place a tortilla in the hot oil and push it down with a ladle to form a bowl. Remove the tortilla when the bowl is lightly browned. Drain the bowls on paper towels.

In each tortilla bowl place ¼ of the lettuce. Sprinkle on the carrots and the alfalfa sprouts.

Add the cucumbers, mushrooms, ham, and cheese.

Artfully arrange the avocado, hard-boiled egg, tomatoes, and black olives on top.

Dribble on the Garden Dressing.

serves 4

"This is like a chef's salad, only it is served in a tortilla shell. This gives it a festive, Southwestern flair."

"You can use Greek olives and goat cheese if you like, which will make it all the better. Vary the ingredients however you want!"

Garden Dressing

1	**large egg yolk**
¼	**cup red wine vinegar**
1	**cup salad oil**
5	**tablespoons Dijon mustard**
1	**pinch salt**
1	**pinch black pepper**

"Don't mix this dressing for too long or else it will start to thicken and turn into a mayonnaise. Just mix it so that it is well blended."

"Our customers really love this dressing! I learned the recipe from an American chef when I was working in San Francisco."

In a small bowl place the egg yolk and whip it.

Add the vinegar and beat it in.

Add the oil and the Dijon mustard. Beat them together until they are well blended and the mixture is smooth.

Add the salt and pepper, and beat them in.

Refrigerate the dressing for 1 hour before using.

Quiche Lorraine

3¼	tablespoons margarine
¼	teaspoon salt
1	tablespoon water
1	egg
½	cup sifted pastry flour
1	tablespoon water
⅔	cup ham, diced
⅔	cup Swiss cheese, grated
5	eggs, lightly beaten
1	pinch salt
1	pinch white pepper
1	pinch nutmeg
4¼	cups half and half

In a small bowl place the margarine, the ¼ teaspoon of salt, and the first 1 tablespoon of water. Cream the ingredients together.

Add the egg and mix it in.

Add the flour and mix it in.

Add the other tablespoon of water and mix it in.

Cover the dough and place it in the refrigerator for 1 hour.

Roll out the dough as thin as possible. Mold the dough in a buttered quiche pan *(it should be 3" high)*.

Preheat the oven to 325°. Place a piece of parchment paper on the bottom of the shell. Fill the pan up with dried beans. Bake the dough for 5 minutes. Remove the dried beans and the paper. Bake the shell for another 5 minutes.

In a small bowl place the ham and Swiss cheese, and mix them together. Sprinkle the ingredients over the bottom of the quiche shell.

In a medium bowl place the remainder of the ingredients. Very gently mix them together.

Pour the mixture into the quiche shell.

Preheat the oven to 325°. Bake the quiche for 40 minutes, or until a knife inserted comes out clean.

serves 4

"This is a classic recipe that was originated in the Lorraine section of France. A lot of people have their own versions of a Quiche Lorraine, but this particular recipe is very close to the original one that was invented many, many years ago."

"Just follow the directions and you won't fail. The dough requires no mixer to make, and you can freeze it without any problem."

"The quiche is very rich because of the cream and eggs. And yet, the taste by itself is very light. It doesn't taste rich at all."

"You may use any kind of pan to cook the quiche in, but it should be at least three inches tall."

"Instead of parchment paper you can use a coffee filter to put under the dried beans."

Taos Chicken Cordon Bleu

4	chicken breasts, skins and bones removed
8	thin slices ham
8	thin slices Swiss cheese
½	cup salsa
¼	cup guacamole
¼	cup green chile peppers, seeded and chopped
4	tablespoons sour cream
2	black olives, pitted and sliced in half

Grill or broil the chicken breasts until they are just done.

Lay 2 slices of ham on top of each chicken breast.

Lay 2 slices of Swiss cheese on top of the ham.

Preheat the oven to 350°. Place the chicken breasts on a flat sheet and bake them for 5 minutes.

On each of 4 individual serving plates place ¼ of the salsa in the center. Place ¼ of the guacamole on top. Sprinkle on ¼ of the green chile peppers. Place the chicken breasts on top.

In the center of each chicken breast place a dollop of sour cream. Place the black olive on top.

serves 4

"Here is a Southwestern version of a classic Chicken Cordon Bleu. It is delicious, and so simple to make! Definitely, this is one of our most popular dishes."

"What is nice about this dish is that you can prepare the chicken several hours ahead, because you heat it up right before you serve it. However, don't keep the chicken in the refrigerator or else that will make it too cold."

"The chicken is lightly spicy, with just a hint of hotness. Serve this with rice and beans, and maybe a fresh vegetable."

Cherry Danish

3   **tablespoons sugar**
3   **tablespoons vegetable shortening**
1   **pinch salt**
1   **large egg, slightly beaten**
¼   **cup pastry flour**
¾   **cup plus 1 tablespoon high gluten flour**
¼   **cup milk**
1½   **tablespoons dry yeast, dissolved in 2 tablespoons**
       warm water
3   **tablespoons butter**
1   **large egg**
2   **tablespoons milk**
½   **cup cherry pie filling**
¼   **cup sugar**
2   **tablespoons milk**
2   **tablespoons butter**

In a medium bowl place the 3 tablespoons of sugar, the shortening, and the salt. Blend the ingredients together.

Slowly add the beaten egg and mix it in.

In a small bowl place the pastry flour and the high gluten flour, and mix them together.

Sift the flour and add it to the egg and shortening mixture. Mix the ingredients together well. Add the ¼ cup of milk and the yeast, and mix them in.

Flatten out the dough on a floured tray and place it in the refrigerator for 1 hour.

Roll the butter into the dough. Flatten the dough out. Fold the dough over three times. Place it in the refrigerator for 2 hours.

Roll out the dough again. Fold it in half. Place it in the refrigerator and leave it there overnight.

Roll out the dough so that it is ½" thick.

Cut the dough into 4 strips. Twist the strips and then shape them into coiled circles.

In a small bowl place the other egg and the first 2 tablespoons of milk. Beat them together to make an egg wash.

(continued on next page)

"I got this recipe from a baker that I used to work with. It's a pastry that comes from Denmark, and it's very, very good!"

"You can make the roll into any creative shape that you want. Use your imagination!"

"Remember, this recipe takes two days to make, because the dough needs to sit in the refrigerator overnight."

"People seem to think this restaurant is a great place to eat after a hard day of skiing. The food is simple, but good, and it's reasonably priced."

Brush the egg wash on top of the coils. Cover the coils with a damp cloth and place them in a warm spot. Let them sit until they rise.

Press the center of each coil down. Fill the centers with the cherry pie filling.

Preheat the oven to 375°. Place the coils on a greased flat sheet and bake them for 15 minutes, or until they are golden brown.

In a small saucepan place the ¼ cup of sugar, the other 2 tablespoons of milk, and the 2 tablespoons of butter. Heat the ingredients until the butter has melted and the sugar is dissolved, to make a glaze.

Brush the rolls with the glaze.

serves 4

Woman Bearing Water, Taos Pueblo, New Mexico

La Cocina de Taos

The festive La Cocina de Taos, with its colorful mural of prominent local citizens from the 1950s, is one of the town's original restaurants. Offering both Mexican and Northern New Mexican dishes, this eatery is popular with everyone!

Owner Jean Sutherland has made few changes to the recipes used in the restaurant almost forty years ago. She says, *"This dish has been used in the restaurant since 1951. Be sure to let the rice brown nicely before you add the liquids. It's not a hot or spicy dish, although some people might like to use green chile peppers instead of the bell peppers, which would certainly make it hotter."*

Sopa de Arroz

2	tablespoons butter
½	cup onions, chopped
1	clove garlic, minced
2	tablespoons green bell peppers, chopped
2	tablespoons celery, chopped
2	tablespoons butter
2	cups long-grain rice
1¾	cups tomato sauce
3	cups chicken stock
1	bay leaf, crumbled
1	teaspoon salt

In a large skillet place the first 2 tablespoons of butter and heat it on medium until it has melted. Add the onions, garlic, bell peppers, and celery. Sauté the ingredients for 2 to 3 minutes, or until the onions are transparent. Remove the vegetables from the skillet.

Place the other 2 tablespoons of butter in the skillet and heat it on medium until it has melted. Add the rice and sauté it for 4 to 5 minutes, or until it is lightly browned.

In a medium large saucepan place the tomato sauce, chicken stock, bay leaf, and salt. Bring the liquid to a boil. Add the sautéed vegetables and the browned rice.

Cover the pan and reduce the heat. Simmer the rice for 25 minutes, or until it is cooked and no longer moist.

serves 8

Sopa de Albondigas

1	pound ground beef
3	slices bread, torn into small pieces
¼	cup milk
1	egg, beaten
¼	teaspoon garlic powder
2	tablespoons dried onion flakes
2	tablespoons fresh cilantro, chopped
2	tablespoons vegetable oil
1½	cups onions, minced
1	clove garlic, minced
2	quarts beef consommé
1	teaspoon chile powder
⅔	cup tomatoes, peeled and chopped
	salt (to taste)
	pepper (to taste)
½	cup fresh cilantro, chopped

"This is a Mexican meatball soup. It's very tasty, and very hearty!"

In a medium bowl place the ground beef, bread, milk, egg, garlic powder, onion flakes, and the 2 tablespoons of cilantro.

Using your hands, mix the ingredients together well.

Shape the meat into small balls. Place them on a cookie sheet.

Preheat the oven to 400°. Bake the meatballs for 30 minutes, or until they are done.

In a small skillet place the oil and heat it on medium until it is hot. Add the onions and garlic, and sauté them for 2 to 3 minutes, or until the onions are translucent.

In a large saucepan place the consommé and bring it to a boil. Reduce the heat to simmer.

Add the meatballs, sautéed onions and garlic, chile powder, tomatoes, salt, and pepper.

Simmer the soup for 30 minutes. Garnish it with the ½ cup of chopped cilantro.

serves 8

"Cilantro is sometimes sold as 'Chinese Parsley' in stores. It has a unique flavor that is hard to duplicate, although you could substitute fresh parsley if necessary. It's very easy to grow in a flower pot in your kitchen, or just scattered outside in your garden."

Chile Colorado con Carne

2½	pounds ground beef
2	teaspoons salt
½	tablespoon garlic powder
½	tablespoon cumin
½	tablespoon caraway seeds
6	tablespoons red chile powder
6	tablespoons paprika
1	cup water
¼	cup tomato sauce

In a large skillet place the meat and sauté it on medium heat until it is done. Drain off the fat.

Add the salt, garlic powder, cumin, caraway seeds, red chile powder, and paprika. Mix everything together well.

Add the water and tomato sauce. Mix them in well.

Simmer the ingredients for 15 minutes.

serves 4

La Cocina Guacamole

1	onion, minced
2	tablespoons vinegar
2	tablespoons peanut oil
1	pinch garlic powder
1	pinch salt
3	large ripe avocados, peeled, seeded, and mashed

In a medium bowl place the onions, vinegar, peanut oil, garlic powder, and salt. Mix the ingredients together well.

Add the mashed avocado and mix it in well.

"This is a very easy dish to make. You can eat it plain, in a bowl, or put it on burritos, enchiladas, or posole. Beans are never used with this chile, and it is very typical in Northern New Mexico."

"New Mexico produces some of the finest chile in the world. It sells for premium prices and is shipped to countries in Europe and Asia. Green chiles can be hot, medium, or mild. Sometimes all three kinds will grow on the same plant! There are chile connoisseurs who can tell the difference between the chiles grown in different areas of New Mexico."

"You can use lemon juice instead of vinegar, which helps to preserve the avocado. Also, you can use olive oil instead of vegetable oil, which changes the flavor."

Tamales

8   **corn husks, opened and cleaned**
2½   **pounds lean pork**
2   **cups water** *(or as needed)*
3   **tablespoons ground red chile**
     salt *(to taste)*
4   **cups masa** *(recipe on next page)*

In a baking pan place the corn husks. Cover them with warm water and let them soak for 2 hours, or until you are ready to use them.

In a medium saucepan place the pork and the water. Simmer the pork for 2 to 3 hours, or until the meat shreds easily with a fork. Add more water if it is needed.

Remove the pork from the saucepan and reserve the stock.

Shred the pork and return it to the stock.

Add the ground red chile and mix it in well. Simmer the meat until all of the liquid is absorbed.

Add the salt and stir it in.

Spread 2 tablespoons of the masa on one half of each corn husk. Place the seasoned, shredded pork on top of the masa. Fold the other half of the husk over the tamale. Roll the husk up. Fold the ends over.

Steam the tamales for 45 minutes *(don't let the water touch the husks)*.

serves 6

"You may use different kinds of fillings in tamales, such as beef, chicken, or turkey. Pork is the most popular in Northern New Mexico."

"Tamales are very versatile. You can make the large ones, or you can make tiny, cocktail bite-size ones. You can pick them up and eat them with your hands, or you can serve them as part of a grand dinner. Eat them plain or serve them with some red chile sauce."

"If you can't find the corn husks you can use foil, but the flavor will be different. Don't use parchment paper.....it won't work. The best idea is to buy some corn husks when you are visiting New Mexico and take them home with you."

Masa

3	cups Masa Harina
1¾	cups pork stock, warmed
1	cup lard
1	teaspoon salt

In a medium bowl place the Masa Harina and the warm pork stock. Let it sit.

In a small bowl place the lard and beat it on medium speed with an electric mixer until it is fluffy and creamy.

Add the salt to the lard and mix it in.

Add the lard to the masa dough and mix it in well.

Salsa de Chile Verde por La Mesa

1½	cups Italian plum tomatoes *(with juice)*, chopped medium
1	cup tomato juice
1	4-ounce can green chile peppers, chopped
1½	tablespoons onions, chopped
¾	tablespoon garlic powder
¾	tablespoon salt
½	tablespoon chile pequin *(crushed red pepper)*
½	cup water *(or as needed)*
	tortilla chips

In a medium saucepan place the chopped tomatoes, tomato juice, green chile peppers, onions, garlic powder, salt, and chile pequin. Mix the ingredients together.

Add enough water to achieve the desired consistency.

Bring the salsa to a boil. Reduce the heat and then simmer it for 2 minutes.

Cool the salsa and then refrigerate it.

Serve the salsa with the tortilla chips.

makes 3 cups

"Masa Harina is a ground cornmeal. It is the essential ingredient to the tamale."

"Tamales are a very traditional Christmas dish. Over the holidays all of the families in Taos make their own special version of tamales and give them to each other."

"Even though this is called 'chile verde', or 'green chile' sauce, it actually is bright red in color. We call it green because of the green chile in it."

"Use this salsa as a dip for chips, or put some on your enchiladas to heat them up. It's wonderful on eggs, and it also serves as a dressing for posole."

Pollo Mole Poblano

6	tablespoons red chile powder
3	tablespoons sesame seeds
¾	cup almonds, slivered and blanched
1	dry corn tortilla, crushed
½	cup seedless raisins
2	cloves garlic
½	teaspoon anise seeds
½	teaspoon ground cinnamon
½	teaspoon powdered cloves
½	teaspoon ground coriander
3	medium, ripe tomatoes, peeled and quartered
2	teaspoons salt
½	teaspoon whole black peppercorns
5	cups chicken stock
1½	ounces unsweetened chocolate, grated
2	broiler chickens, halved

In a medium bowl place the red chile powder, sesame seeds, almonds, crushed tortilla, raisins, garlic, anise seeds, cinnamon, cloves, coriander, tomatoes, salt, peppercorns, and 2 cups of the chicken stock.

Mix the ingredients together and pour them into a blender. Purée the mixture until it is a thick paste.

Place the other 3 cups of chicken stock in a medium large sauce pan and heat it. While stirring constantly, gradually add the blended paste. Bring the sauce to a boil.

Reduce the heat and add the chocolate.

Simmer the sauce until the chocolate has melted and a thick gravy is formed.

In a large saucepan, half filled with boiling water, place the chicken. Reduce the heat, cover, and simmer the chicken for 15 minutes.

Broil the chicken for 5 to 10 minutes on each side, or until it is nicely browned. Serve it with the sauce.

serves 4

"This is a great recipe because it has so many ingredients in it, and it's really a lot of fun to put together. Just make certain that you don't leave out any of the ingredients."

"If people aren't familiar with the mole sauce, then we will give them a taste first, because it is usually a love or hate affair!"

"You can make the sauce in advance and then freeze it."

Chile Rellenos

12	**green chile peppers, roasted, peeled, and seeded** *(see chef's comments on this page for roasting instructions)*
12	**1" thick fingers of cheddar cheese, the length of the chile peppers**
⅔	**cup flour** *(or as needed)*
⅓	**cup bread crumbs**
½	**teaspoon salt**
5	**eggs, lightly beaten**
1¼	**cups milk**
¼	**cup vegetable oil**

Place one finger of cheese in each green chile pepper.

In a small bowl place the flour, bread crumbs, and salt. Mix the ingredients together.

In another small bowl place the eggs and milk, and mix them together.

In a large skillet place the oil and heat it on medium until it is hot.

Dip the stuffed chiles into the flour mixture, then into the egg mixture, and again into the flour mixture.

Lightly fry the stuffed chiles on each side until they are nicely browned and the cheese is melted.

serves 4

"Chile rellenos are great for breakfast, lunch, or dinner. You can use different kinds of cheeses in them, and the chiles can be fresh or canned."

"You may grill the chile rellenos instead of frying them, and they will be that much healthier."

"To roast and peel chile peppers is easy. Lightly brush them with oil and then place them under a preheated broiler, with the door open (wear rubber gloves). Turn them frequently until the skins begin to blacken and blister. Remove the peppers from the oven and then wrap them in a damp towel. Let them sit for ten minutes. The skins should peel off very easily. You also can blacken the skins over an open flame, or over hot coals. Don't rub your eyes with your hands!"

Saint Jerome Church, Taos Pueblo, New Mexico

Lambert's of Taos

Serving New American Cuisine in a warm, hospitable, renovated house, Lambert's is the latest addition to the fine restaurants of Taos. With its high standard of quality in food preparation and service, this attractive new eating establishment is destined to become a local favorite.

Owners Zeke and Tina Lambert have fulfilled a long-time dream with the creation of their lovely restaurant. Zeke is both the chef and the creator of these recipes.

"This is a variation on the traditional wilted spinach salad. It has a wonderful, slightly sweet and sour taste."

Spinach Salad with Prosciutto

2	large bunches spinach, stemmed, cleaned, and dried
4	ounces prosciutto, thinly julienned
	black pepper *(to taste)*
¾	cup walnut oil
½	red onion, julienned
½	cup walnut pieces
¼	cup raspberry vinegar
4	tablespoons Parmesan cheese, freshly grated

In a large bowl place the spinach, prosciutto, and black pepper. Toss the ingredients together.

In a medium skillet place the walnut oil and heat it on medium until it is hot. Add the onions and sauté them for 30 seconds, or until they are wilted but not brown.

Remove the skillet from the heat. Add the walnuts and toss them.

Add the raspberry vinegar and stir it in slightly.

Immediately pour the dressing over the spinach and toss it so that the leaves are well coated.

Arrange the spinach on individual serving plates. Have the majority of the prosciutto, walnuts, and onions on top.

Sprinkle on the Parmesan cheese.

serves 4

Lime Marinated Scallops
with Jicama Chile Salad

½   **pound scallops, cleaned**
3   **tablespoons lime juice, freshly squeezed**
1   **medium jicama, peeled and julienned**
½   **green bell pepper, julienned**
½   **red onion, julienned**
¼   **teaspoon red chile powder**
½   **cup light oil**
2   **tablespoons lime juice, freshly squeezed**
4   **sprigs cilantro, chopped**
     salt *(to taste)*
     pepper *(to taste)*
1   **head leaf lettuce, cleaned and dried**

In a medium bowl place the scallops and the 3 tablespoons of lime juice. Gently toss the scallops so that they are well coated. Let them marinate for 1 hour.

In a medium bowl place the jicama, bell peppers, onions, and chile powder. Gently toss the ingredients together.

Add the oil, the 2 tablespoons of lime juice, the cilantro, salt, and pepper. Gently toss the ingredients together.

Take enough of the leaf lettuce to cover one half of 4 individual serving plates, and toss it with the jicama mixture so that it is well coated with the dressing.

Remove the lettuce and place it on one half of each serving plate. Place the jicama mixture on top of the lettuce. Place the scallops on the other half of each plate.

Dribble a few drops of the dressing on top of the scallops.

serves 4

"Essentially this recipe is a combination of different ideas. The delicate flavor of the scallops contrasts nicely with the crisp and spicy nature of the Jicama Chile Salad."

"The scallops must be very fresh for this recipe to work. I would recommend staying away from the frozen ones."

"When you julienne the vegetables try to make everything the same size."

Zeke's Easy Potatoes

6	**large red potatoes, diced into ¾" cubes**
½	**cup vegetable oil**
1	**tablespoon salt**
	pepper *(to taste)*

Preheat the oven to 300°.

Place the potatoes on a cookie sheet. Sprinkle them with the oil and the salt. Toss them so that they are well coated.

Bake the potatoes for 30 to 40 minutes, or until they are brown and crispy on the outside, and tender on the inside. Turn them occasionally so that they are re-coated with the oil.

Grind on the pepper.

serves 6

"These potatoes are really delicious. People are always asking, 'How in the world did you make these?' And they are so easy to make!"

"My favorite dishes are those with simple flavors, and I like working to make the most out of these flavors. I tend to stay away from complex recipes, especially those with a large number of ingredients, because I don't want to have the flavors competing with each other. Rather, I look for a contrast of flavors and textures. But most of all, I look for a balance in flavor and texture. Balance in food, just as in life, is good!"

Grilled Chicken Breast and Sausage with Blue Corn Polenta and Pico de Gallo

Grilled Chicken Breast and Sausage

4   chicken thighs, skin removed, boned, and cubed
2   strips bacon, diced
1   tablespoon green peppercorns
2   tablespoons white wine
2   teaspoons salt
2   chicken breasts, skin removed, boned, and halved
     Blue Corn Polenta (recipe on next page)
     Pico de Gallo (recipe on next page)

In a medium bowl place the cubed chicken, bacon, peppercorns, white wine, and salt. Mix the ingredients together. Let the chicken marinate for 4 to 6 hours.

In a food processor place part of the marinated chicken mixture. Using short bursts, chop the chicken so that it is in small pea-size pieces. Place it in a medium bowl. Repeat the process for the remainder of the chicken.

Gently stir the mixture so that everything is well incorporated.

Pack the sausage into 4 small, individual soufflé dishes. Place them in a baking dish half filled with hot water.

Preheat the oven to 325°. Bake the sausage for 20 minutes, or until it is firm, but not browned.

Grill the marinated chicken breasts and the sausage over hot coals until they are done.

Serve the chicken and sausage with the Blue Corn Polenta and the Pico de Gallo.

serves 4

"This is very French! It utilizes the French technique of taking a fowl and making a sausage out of one part of it, and then cooking the sausage with the other, most succulent part."

"The polenta is Italian, and the Pico de Gallo is a spicy Mexican condiment. So, we are trying to come up with a new Southwestern food using indigenous ingredients, but also using techniques and dishes from other countries."

"The sausage may seem difficult, but it really is quite simple. Just remember not to over-process the chicken. It should not be puréed so that it is smooth, like a frankfurter. And, be sure not to over-bake it in the oven. You should cook it just to the point where it holds together."

Blue Corn Polenta

2	**cups chicken stock** *(or as needed)*
1	**teaspoon salt**
3	**tablespoons butter**
2	**cups blue cornmeal**
½	**pound Monterey Jack cheese, grated**

In a medium saucepan place the chicken stock, salt, and butter. Bring the liquid to a boil.

Add the cornmeal and stir it constantly until it bubbles. Add more broth if necessary.

Reduce the heat and cook the polenta for 5 to 10 minutes, or until the consistency is very thick and grainy.

Spread the polenta on a baking sheet so that it is ½" thick.

Refrigerate it for 2 hours.

Cut the polenta into triangles.

Grill the polenta for 3 to 5 minutes on each side, or until it is heated through. After the polenta is flipped over, sprinkle the cheese on top.

serves 4

Pico de Gallo

3	**medium tomatoes, chopped and drained**
1	**clove garlic, minced**
1	**jalapeño pepper, seeded and finely diced**
½	**red onion, diced**
2	**tablespoons cilantro, chopped**
2	**tablespoons lime juice, freshly squeezed**
½	**teaspoon salt**
¼	**teaspoon pepper**

In a medium bowl place all of the ingredients and mix them together well.

Let the mixture sit for 1 hour before serving.

"In Italian cooking, when they make the polenta it is really a slow process, and it is cooked to a smooth and creamy porridge consistency. However, with the blue corn, our goal is to emphasize the grainy texture, as well as the really outstanding flavor. I try to find local blue corn that has been organically grown and then we grind it fresh every day. Unfortunately, the majority of people in America aren't able to do this. I guess this is one of the advantages of living in Taos! Of course, you can use yellow corn, and it will be perfectly fine."

"The Pico de Gallo should be made and eaten in the same day. In fact, for that really crisp and crunchy texture, you shouldn't let it sit for more than several hours."

"The jalapeños vary tremendously in how hot they are. The seeds are the hottest part, so to reduce the hotness you can seed the pepper and then mince it really fine. Then, go according to your taste. If you are really hard core you can add up to three peppers!"

Marinated Grilled Pork Tenderloin
with **Green Chile Glaze**
and **Apple Onion Relish**

Marinated Grilled Pork Tenderloin
with **Green Chile Glaze**

½   cup green chile peppers, finely chopped
3   tablespoons honey
¼   cup light vegetable oil
½   cup chicken stock
3   cloves garlic, minced
2   pounds pork tenderloin
    Apple Onion Relish *(recipe on next page)*

In a large bowl place the green chile peppers, honey, oil, chicken stock, and garlic. Mix everything together well.

Add the pork and coat it with the marinade. Cover the pork and refrigerate it for 4 hours. Turn it occasionally.

Remove the pork and set it aside.

Strain the marinade through a fine sieve into a small saucepan. Bring the marinade to a boil and then reduce the heat. Simmer the liquid for 15 to 20 minutes, or until it is reduced to a light glaze *(it will lightly coat a spoon)*.

Grill the pork to the desired doneness. Let it rest for 10 minutes.

Slice the pork on the bias into ¼" thick medallions.

Place ½ cup of the Apple Onion Relish in the center of 4 individual serving plates.

Artfully arrange the pork medallions around the relish.

Reheat the glaze and pour it over each serving of the meat.

serves 4

"I probably have been doing this recipe in one form or another for ten or twelve years. The green chile glaze is an addition that we do in Taos because it gives it a nice Southwestern hit! However, you don't need the glaze to make this recipe work. You can just use the Apple Onion Relish with pork chops, and it's great!"

"Pork tenderloins vary in size quite a bit, so buy one and one half pounds to two pounds. You are going to slice the pork after it is cooked, so it is not really important exactly how much you buy."

"As a general rule, it is good to let meat sit for ten minutes or so after it is cooked. This gives time for the juices to settle back into the meat, and you will have a more consistent doneness throughout."

"Serve this dish with Zeke's Easy Potatoes!"

*"I feel that apples,
onions, and potatoes have
a wonderful affinity for
each other, and the
possibilities for their
different combinations are
endless."*

*"If the relish is too sweet
at the end, then the flavor
will be 'blah', so you will
need to add some vinegar.
What you need is the
proper balance, so be
sure to taste it before you
serve it."*

Apple Onion Relish

3   **tablespoons butter**
2   **medium onions, julienned**
4   **tart apples, cored, peeled, and sliced**
      apple cider vinegar *(to taste)*

In a medium saucepan place the butter and heat it on
medium high until it has melted. Add the onions and sauté
them for 5 to 7 minutes, or until they are slightly caramelized.

Add the apples. Reduce the heat and cook the apples for 1
hour, or until they are tender and the mixture is of a relish
consistency. Stir the relish occasionally.

Add the vinegar if necessary, so that the desired tartness is
achieved.

Velarde Apple Tart

1	teaspoon sugar
½	teaspoon salt
2	tablespoons butter
½	large egg, lightly beaten
2	tablespoons milk
1	cup flour
1	cup milk
1	vanilla bean, split
¾	cup heavy cream
4	eggs
¾	cup sugar
3	cups tart apples, peeled, cored, and thinly sliced
1½	tablespoons butter
3	tablespoons sugar

In a medium bowl place the 1 teaspoon of sugar, salt, and the 2 tablespoons of butter. Cream the ingredients together until they have a smooth consistency.

Add the ½ egg and the 2 tablespoons of milk. Mix them in well.

Add the flour and mix it in well. The dough should have a smooth consistency *(do not over-mix)*. Cover the dough and refrigerate it for 1 hour.

Roll out the dough on a floured board.

Place the dough in a buttered and floured 9" pie pan. Prick the bottom with a fork.

Place a piece of parchment paper on top of the dough. Fill the pan with dried beans.

Preheat the oven to 350°. Bake the tart shell for 15 to 20 minutes, or until it is half done. Remove the dried beans and parchment paper. Let the tart shell cool.

In a small saucepan place the 1 cup of milk and the vanilla bean. Heat the milk on medium until it comes to a boil. Let it boil for 1 minute and then remove it from the heat. Remove the vanilla bean.

Add the cream to the milk and stir it in.

In a medium bowl place the 4 eggs and the ¾ cup of sugar. Beat them together until the mixture is smooth.

(continued on next page)

"Velarde is a town on the Rio Grande River between Taos and Santa Fe. It is traditionally an apple and chile growing area. In fact, I believe that it is the apple center of New Mexico. In the fall the apples are wonderful!"

"This flan recipe works very well with fruit. When you arrange the apples in the bottom of the pie shell be sure that you pack them in tightly so that there are no air holes."

While stirring constantly, slowly add the milk mixture until it is well incorporated.

While stirring constantly, place the bowl in a larger bowl filled with ice water. Continue to stir the mixture for 5 to 10 minutes, or until it is cool and smooth. Set it aside.

In the bottom of the pie shell arrange the apple slices in overlapping, concentric circles. The bottom should be completely covered, with no air gaps.

Pour in the flan until it is ¼" from the top of the crust.

Dot the top with the 1½ tablespoons of butter.

Preheat the oven to 350°. Bake the flan for 20 minutes. Sprinkle the top with the 3 tablespoons of sugar.

Bake it for another 15 to 20 minutes, or until the apples are tender and the flan is set.

serves 8

"There are a lot of steps to this recipe. However, the result is so outstanding that it is really worth the effort!"

Chocolate Mousse

7	ounces semi-sweet chocolate
½	cup butter
3	egg yolks
5	egg whites
1½	cups sugar

Melt the chocolate and the butter in a double boiler, and then remove it from the heat.

Add the egg yolks and mix them in well.

In a medium bowl place the egg whites. Beat them until they form stiff peaks. Halfway through the process add the sugar.

Fold the chocolate mixture into the egg whites.

Cover the mousse and refrigerate it for 2 hours, or until it is set.

serves 6

"The most important thing is that you don't burn the chocolate, which is a very easy thing to do. Using a double boiler is a safe method of melting it. Or, if you're doing a lot of cooking and your oven is hot, you can put the chocolate in a ceramic bowl and place it on the back part of the stove. Some people claim that melting the chocolate in a microwave is absolutely foolproof. If you use this method, then I recommend using ten second blasts."

"This mousse works wonderfully as a straight dessert. It is great with a raspberry sauce and a hazelnut cookie. It also is good with Crème Anglaise, which is a vanilla sauce."

Wagon Wheel, Millicent Rogers Museum, Taos, New Mexico

Michael's Kitchen

Michael's Kitchen is one of those special places where one can relax for hours, sipping coffee and chatting with friends. The cheerful staff serves simple, homemade dishes that are loved by both locals and tourists.

Owner Michael Ninneman says, *"Hoop cheese is hard to find, but you should be able to get it in a gourmet store. If not, you can substitute Ricotta, which is similar."*

"These blintzes are smooth, rich, and delicious. If you really want to hurt yourself, then you can add some cinnamon and raisins!"

Michael's Blintzes

½ cup hoop cheese
½ cup cottage cheese
⅓ cup sour cream
2 tablespoons sugar
1 teaspoon oil
Crêpe Batter *(see page 133)*
2 tablespoons powdered sugar
1 cup strawberries, quartered
4 tablespoons sour cream

In a small bowl place the hoop cheese, cottage cheese, the ⅓ cup of sour cream, and the sugar. Mix the ingredients together until they are well blended and creamy.

Place the mixture in a pastry bag.

In a small sauté pan place the oil and heat it on medium until it is hot. While stirring the batter, pour some of it into the sauté pan. Cook it briefly until the top appears to be dry. Turn the crêpe over and cook the other side for 5 seconds. Remove the crêpe and repeat the process until 8 crêpes are made *(extra batter may be frozen)*.

Pipe the blintz filling onto each crêpe. Roll the crêpes up and dust them with the powdered sugar.

Garnish the crêpes with the strawberries and sour cream.

serves 4

Banana Nut Pancakes
with Banana Syrup

Banana Nut Pancakes

1½	**cups flour**
1	**teaspoon baking powder**
3	**tablespoons sugar**
1	**teaspoon salt**
2	**eggs, lightly beaten**
3	**tablespoons butter, melted**
1⅓	**cups milk**
¼	**cup Durkees banana crystals**
2	**tablespoons vegetable oil**
¼	**cup pecans, chopped**
1	**tablespoon powdered sugar**
1	**banana, peeled and sliced**
	Banana Syrup *(recipe on next page)*

In a medium bowl place the flour, baking powder, sugar, and salt. Mix the ingredients together.

Add the eggs, butter, and milk. Lightly mix the ingredients together *(do not over-mix)*.

Add the banana crystals and gently mix them in.

Cover the batter and refrigerate it overnight.

In a large skillet place the vegetable oil and heat it on medium until it is hot. Drop spoonfuls of the batter in the skillet. Sprinkle on some of the nuts. Fry the pancakes on each side until they are golden brown.

Dust the pancakes with the powdered sugar.

Serve the pancakes with the banana slices and the Banana Syrup.

serves 4

"I use freeze-dried banana crystals. If you can't find them, then try dried bananas instead. Banana flavoring from the grocery store won't work because it has alcohol in it."

"Be sure not to over-mix the batter. There should be little chunks of flour in it."

"These pancakes are very rich and very sweet. They are great if you are really into sweet tastes. Many people will eat up to four, but personally, I can eat only two of them."

"You can add blueberries to the batter and have blueberry pancakes. Or, you can add some cocoa and have chocolate pancakes. Pancakes are very versatile. You can add just about anything that you want."

"The people of Taos have accepted Michael's Kitchen and have made it a part of Taos. They have been very good to us and we will always be grateful."

"This is just a basic, simple syrup with banana crystals. It complements the banana nut pancakes, which are incredibly popular at the restaurant."

"At Michael's Kitchen we have a full bakery, and our bakery items are well loved. There is a man from Denver who will call me every so often and announce that he's coming to Taos and that I should have an extra thirty loaves of my banana nut bread ready. He literally fills up his trunk with the bread, drives back to Denver, and freezes them! And, we are always sending items to people in other states by UPS."

"We make a Poor Man's Eggs Benedict, which people really love. You take an English muffin, cut it in half, lay on a piece of ham, and eggs that are prepared to your taste. Then you smother it with green chile and top it with cheese. It tastes delicious and takes no time to make."

Banana Syrup

1	**cup water**
½	**cup sugar**
¼	**cup Durkees banana crystals**

In a small saucepan place the water and bring it to a boil. Add the sugar and stir it in.

Let the syrup cool.

Add the banana crystals and stir them in.

Heat the syrup before serving.

Crêpe Batter

¾	**cup all purpose flour**
½	**teaspoon salt**
½	**teaspoon baking powder**
2	**tablespoons sugar**
2	**eggs, beaten**
1	**cup milk**
⅓	**cup butter, melted**

In a medium bowl place all of the ingredients and beat them together with an electric mixer until the batter is frothy.

Cover the batter and refrigerate it for 24 hours.

Stir the batter before using it.

makes 16 crêpes

Strawberry Crêpes

2   **cups strawberries, quartered**
1   **cup sugar**
1   **teaspoon oil**
    Crêpe Batter *(recipe on previous page)*
2   **tablespoons powdered sugar**
4   **tablespoons sour cream**

In a medium bowl place the strawberries. Add the sugar and stir it in. Place the strawberries in the refrigerator for 6 to 8 hours.

Remove the strawberries and place them in a medium saucepan. Quickly bring them to a boil and then reduce the heat to low. Simmer the strawberries briefly until they are heated.

In a small sauté pan place the oil and heat it on medium until it is hot. While stirring the batter, pour some of it into the sauté pan. Cook it briefly until the top appears to be dry. Turn the crêpe over and cook the other side for 5 seconds. Remove the crêpe and repeat the process until 8 crêpes are made *(extra batter may be frozen)*.

Place the heated strawberries inside the crêpes and roll them up.

Dust the crêpes with the powdered sugar. Spoon on some of the remaining strawberries. Garnish the crêpes with a dollop of sour cream.

serves 4

"The Strawberry Crêpes are very easy to make. The hardest part is learning to physically deal with the crêpes, which is just a question of getting the knack of how to cook them."

"We always dust our crêpes and blintzes with powdered sugar and then serve them with some sour cream. This makes the presentation really nice."

"When a customer comes to our restaurant I want him to enjoy the place, and get a good value for his money. There's nothing I personally hate more than the feeling of being taken to the cleaners. I just hate it! When that happens to me I never forget it!"

Michael's Potato Pancakes

2	cups potatoes, grated
3	eggs, well beaten
1	tablespoon onions, grated
1½	tablespoons flour
½	teaspoon baking powder
1¼	teaspoons salt
1	teaspoon pepper
¼	cup vegetable oil
2	cups vegetable oil
1	cup apple sauce
½	cup sour cream

In a medium bowl place the grated potatoes, eggs, onions, flour, baking powder, salt, and pepper. Mix the ingredients together well.

Place the mixture in the refrigerator and let it sit for 24 hours.

Place the mixture in a colander and let it drain.

Pat the potato mixture into patties that are ½" thick and 3" in diameter.

In a large skillet place the ¼ cup of vegetable oil and heat it on medium high until it is hot. Add the potato pancakes and quickly sear them on each side until they are golden brown.

In a medium saucepan place the 2 cups of oil and heat it on high until it is hot. Deep-fry the potato pancakes so that they are crispy. Drain them on paper towels.

Serve the potato pancakes with the apple sauce and a large dollop of sour cream.

serves 4

"The secret as to why these taste so good is that the potatoes sit for a day or two, and all the water drains out. This makes the texture really excellent."

"Another great, easy dish that we make is a Tortilla Rellaña, which is actually a breakfast burrito. You take minced ham, chives, and scrambled eggs. Roll them up in a flour tortilla and then smother it with green chile sauce. We serve it with hash browns to satisfy our potato fans, but I think it's better with chopped lettuce and tomatoes."

Detail, Cabot Plaza Mall, Taos, New Mexico

Ogelvie's

Ogelvie's restaurant offers a winning combination – sumptuous food in one of the most charming locations in Taos. Here people can enjoy the fresh and original dishes on the pleasant balcony overlooking the historic plaza.

Menu

Fiesta Bowl

Chicken Chile Soup

Sliced Grilled Chicken Salad

Chicken Pasta Salad Cashew Sauce

Grilled Shrimp and Feta Cheese Pasta Salad

Baked Mostaccioli with Italian Sausage

Salmon Ricotta Ravioli Walnut Cream Sauce

Linguini and Bay Scallops in Orange Ginger Cream

Pollo Verde

Ricotta and Prosciutto Cannelloni

Ogelvie's Grilled Salmon Pesto Cream Linguini

Grilled Chicken and Vegetable Fettucini

Ogelvie's Adobe Pie

Owner Roger Roessler offers this appetizer as an alternative to the traditional nachos. His one comment is, *"It's a great party dish!"*

Fiesta Bowl

½   pound lean ground beef
¼   cup onions, diced
¼   teaspoon garlic, minced
⅛   teaspoon coriander
⅛   teaspoon cumin
⅛   cup tomato salsa
1   cup refried beans
¾   cup cheddar cheese, grated
¾   cup Monterey Jack cheese, grated
¼   cup sour cream
¼   cup guacamole
2   cups oil
12 corn tortillas, cut into wedges
    salt *(to taste)*
1   cup tomato salsa

In a medium skillet place the ground beef, onions, garlic, coriander, and cumin *(add a little oil if needed)*. Sauté the ingredients until the beef is cooked. Strain off the grease. Add the ⅛ cup of salsa and mix it in.

Preheat the oven to 350°. In a 3" deep baking dish place the beef. Smooth the refried beans on top. Sprinkle on the two cheeses. Bake the casserole for 30 minutes.

Spread on the sour cream and guacamole.

In a large skillet place the oil and heat it on medium high until it is hot. Quickly fry the tortilla wedges until they are golden brown. Drain them on paper towels. Sprinkle on the salt.

Serve the casserole with the chips and the 1 cup of salsa on the side.

serves 4

Chicken Chile Soup

1	**3-pound whole chicken**
1	**gallon water**
1	**teaspoon salt**
½	**teaspoon pepper**
4	**tablespoons butter**
3	**cups celery, diced**
1	**cup carrots, diced**
1	**cup onions, diced**
2	**cups canned green chile peppers, diced**
2	**cups heavy cream**
	salt *(to taste)*
	pepper *(to taste)*
½	**cup cornstarch, dissolved in water**

In a large stock pot place the chicken, water, salt, and pepper. Bring the liquid to a boil and then reduce the heat to low. Simmer the chicken for 3 hours, or until it is so tender that it falls apart.

Remove the chicken and reserve the broth.

Skin and de-bone the chicken. Coarsely chop the meat.

In a large sauté pan place the butter and heat it on medium until it has melted. Add the celery, carrots, and onions. Sauté the vegetables for 5 minutes, or until they are tender.

Bring the reserved chicken broth to a boil and then reduce the heat. Add the sautéed vegetables, green chile peppers, and heavy cream. Season the soup with the salt and pepper.

While stirring constantly, slowly add the cornstarch mixture so that the desired consistency is achieved.

Add the chicken and stir it in.

serves 4

"It seems like there are a lot of recipes out there for a chile chicken soup, and this is our version. Years ago we tried to make a different soup every single day, and this was one of them. But, it was so popular that we decided to serve it one day every single week. So, now this is our Tuesday soup!"

"The recipe is very easy. You don't have to buy a whole chicken and cook it if you don't have time. You can just buy some boneless chicken breasts, chop them up, sauté them, and throw them in the soup. However, if you do take the trouble to cook the whole chicken and make your own broth, then the flavor will be better. But, this is always true when you are making something from scratch."

"The only trick here is in the thickening of the soup. It is really up to the individual to determine how thick he or she wants it, so the amount of the cornstarch mixture that is added may vary quite a bit from one person to another. Personally, I don't like the soup to be too thick. Also, remember that the soup will thicken more the longer it cooks."

"I came up with this recipe when we were designing some dishes that we call 'light and healthy'. This particular recipe has been approved by the American Heart Association."

"I don't think that the salad is complete without the red bell peppers. There was a food critic who reviewed this dish and he had the same opinion. For some reason, the red bell peppers really make the dish come together."

"We use Wish-Bone Italian Dressing on our house salad along with some freshly grated Parmesan cheese and toasted sesame seeds. Now, you may be disapproving that we use a commercially bottled dressing, but there is a true story behind the reason. My partner and I occasionally used to eat at this really exclusive club in Phoenix. We both went crazy over their salad, it was so good! Finally we decided to call up the chef, and he was nice enough to tell us that they used plain ol' Wish-Bone. You won't believe how many compliments we get on our salads!"

Sliced Grilled Chicken Salad

4	5-ounce chicken breasts, skin and bones removed
½	cup olive oil
2	tablespoons fresh rosemary, chopped
1	head Romaine lettuce, washed, soaked in ice water, dried, and torn
2	medium red bell peppers, cored, washed, and sliced into rings
1	cucumber, sliced
	Wish-Bone Italian Dressing
⅛	cup Romano cheese, freshly grated
2	teaspoons sesame seeds, toasted

In a shallow dish place the chicken breasts. Drizzle on the olive oil. Sprinkle on the fresh rosemary. Cover the chicken and let it marinate for 2 to 3 hours.

In a large bowl place the Romaine lettuce, bell peppers, and cucumber. Sprinkle on some Wish-Bone Italian Dressing and toss the salad well.

Add the Romano cheese and the toasted sesame seeds, and toss them in well.

Remove the marinated chicken with a slotted spoon and let it drain.

Grill the chicken for 3 to 4 minutes on each side, or until it is cooked. Slice the chicken diagonally into ½" strips.

On 4 chilled, individual salad plates place the Romaine lettuce. Arrange the bell peppers and cucumber slices around each plate.

Place the grilled chicken on top.

serves 4

Ogelvie's

Chicken Pasta Salad
in Cashew Sauce

Chicken Pasta Salad

1	pound chicken breasts, skin removed, boned, and cubed medium
½	cup pineapple juice
½	cup Kikkoman Teriyaki Sauce
¼	cup water
1	pound linguini, cooked al dente, drained, and chilled
2	oranges, thinly sliced
1	cucumber, sliced
¼	cup cashews, chopped
	Cashew Sauce *(recipe on next page)*
½	cup scallions, chopped
¼	cup sesame seeds, toasted

In a medium saucepan place the chicken, pineapple juice, teriyaki sauce, and water. Simmer the chicken for 30 minutes *(do not boil)*. Remove the chicken with a slotted spoon. Reserve the broth for the Cashew Sauce.

On 4 individual chilled serving platters place the linguini.

Lay the orange and cucumber slices along one side, in an alternating pattern.

Place the chicken on top of the linguini.

Sprinkle on the cashew pieces.

Ladle on the Cashew Sauce.

Sprinkle on the scallions and the toasted sesame seeds.

serves 4

"This salad is like an Oriental dish with a Southwestern kick to it!"

"Keep the chicken in its cooking liquid until you are ready to serve it..... otherwise it will dry out."

"You will have to toast the sesame seeds yourself, but that is very easy to do. Just spread some on a flat baking sheet, put them in the oven, and when they start to turn brown, take them out. The flavor changes dramatically when you toast them."

"The cucumber and orange slices make a nice garnish visually, and when you pour the Cashew Sauce over them they taste really great!"

"I have another Ogelvie's in Santa Fe, and the Old Timer's Cafes in Albuquerque and Durango. Someday I hope to open another Ogelvie's in Albuquerque."

Cashew Sauce

1	**cup chicken-pineapple-teriyaki broth** *(from Chicken Pasta Salad – recipe on previous page)*
¼	**cup red wine vinegar**
¼	**cup sesame oil**
½	**cup water**
½	**cup pineapple juice**
½	**teaspoon garlic, minced**
½	**teaspoon fresh ginger, grated**
¼	**teaspoon crushed red peppers**
2	**tablespoons corn starch, dissolved in 2 tablespoons water**
½	**cup cashews**

In a medium saucepan place all of the ingredients except for the corn starch and cashews. Simmer the mixture for 30 minutes.

Bring the liquid to a boil. While stirring constantly, add the corn starch to thicken the sauce.

Simmer the sauce for 30 minutes.

Strain the sauce through a fine sieve.

Set the sauce aside until it is cool. Place it in the refrigerator so that it chills.

Add the cashews just before you are ready to serve the sauce.

"The sauce takes a little bit of time to make, so it probably is not the kind of thing that you want to make right after you get home from work. But the nice thing about this recipe is that you can prepare the sauce ahead of time, and then the rest is easy to do."

"Usually during the summer months we will offer three or four salads, and then in the winter we will replace them with heartier dishes. However, the Chicken Pasta Salad in Cashew Sauce stays on the menu all year long because people would be too upset if we took it off."

"We offer some really excellent dishes that one could almost call gourmet, except that we do them in a casual atmosphere at reasonable prices."

Grilled Shrimp and Feta Cheese Pasta Salad

1	pound medium shrimp, shelled and deveined
4	tablespoons olive oil
2	tablespoons lime juice, freshly squeezed
1	cup plum tomatoes, chopped
½	cup black olives, pitted
6	ounces feta cheese
1	pound medium pasta shells, cooked al dente and chilled
½	cup fresh basil, torn into pieces
½	cup balsamic vinegar
4	tablespoons olive oil
1	teaspoon sugar
	salt *(to taste)*
	pepper *(to taste)*
4	sprigs fresh basil

In a medium bowl place the shrimp, the first 4 tablespoons of olive oil, and the lime juice. Marinate the shrimp for 3 hours.

Grill the shrimp for 3 to 4 minutes on each side, or until they are done. Place the shrimp in the refrigerator for 45 minutes, or until they are chilled.

In a large bowl place the chilled shrimp, tomatoes, olives, feta cheese, pasta shells, and the torn basil leaves. Mix the ingredients together.

In a small bowl place the balsamic vinegar, the other 4 tablespoons of olive oil, the sugar, salt, and pepper. Whip the ingredients together until they are well blended.

Add the vinaigrette to the pasta and toss it in well.

Garnish the pasta salad with the fresh basil sprigs.

serves 4

"There are various different powerful tastes in this recipe, such as the balsamic vinegar, feta cheese, basil, and the grilled shrimp. However, they all blend together in such a way that they create an exquisite flavor!"

"Even though I am not a professionally trained chef, I love to be in the kitchen and experiment with different foods. I think that I have a certain feel for putting things together. However, I must confess that at times I do get into trouble, and so I have to look to the other guys for help!"

Baked Mostaccioli with Italian Sausage

2	tablespoons vegetable oil
1	pound sweet, bulk Italian sausage
2	tablespoons butter
2	tablespoons flour
1	cup heavy cream
⅛	teaspoon nutmeg
	salt *(to taste)*
	white pepper *(to taste)*
2	cups marinara sauce, heated
1	tablespoon olive oil
1	teaspoon garlic, diced
1	green bell pepper, roasted, peeled, seeded, and julienned
1	red bell pepper, roasted, peeled, seeded, and julienned
1	pound mostaccioli, cooked al dente
2	cups Mozzarella cheese, grated

In a large skillet place the vegetable oil and heat it on medium until it is hot. Add the Italian sausage and cook it until it is done. Drain off the grease and set it aside.

In a medium saucepan place the butter and heat it on medium until it has melted. Add the flour and stir it in. While stirring constantly, cook the roux for 2 to 3 minutes.

Reduce the heat to low. While stirring constantly, slowly add the heavy cream and cook the sauce for 4 to 5 minutes. Add the nutmeg, salt, and white pepper, and stir them in.

Add the white sauce to the marinara sauce and stir it in well.

In a large skillet place the olive oil and heat it on medium until it is hot. Add the garlic and roasted bell peppers, and sauté them for 2 to 3 minutes.

In a large bowl place the cooked mostaccioli, roasted bell peppers, Italian sausage, and tomato cream sauce. Mix the ingredients together.

In a medium baking dish place the mostaccioli mixture. Sprinkle on the Mozzarella cheese.

Preheat the oven to 375°. Bake the casserole for 25 minutes.

serves 4

"The mostaccioli is a big, round noodle that I remember having as a little boy, when my mom would use it in casseroles. I think that it is a pasta that most people will relate to. Some of the newer pastas that are appearing on menus may seem so foreign that people don't even know what they are."

"This is another one of those great dishes that will please almost anybody. It's the perfect dish for a potluck or a party."

"My philosophy of cooking is that you should use the freshest ingredients that are available, and don't complicate things!"

Salmon Ricotta Ravioli
with Walnut Cream Sauce

Salmon Ricotta Ravioli

¾   cup salmon, cooked and flaked
1½   cups Ricotta cheese
2   egg yolks
⅛   teaspoon nutmeg
⅛   teaspoon white pepper
40   3" by 3" pasta squares, uncooked
2   eggs, beaten
4   quarts water
1   teaspoon salt
      Walnut Cream Sauce (recipe on next page)
½   cup Parmesan cheese, freshly grated

In a medium bowl place the flaked salmon, Ricotta cheese, egg yolks, nutmeg, and white pepper. Combine the ingredients together well.

In the center of one pasta square place 2 tablespoons of the filling. Brush the beaten eggs on the edges of the pasta square around the filling.

Place another pasta square on top. Pinch the edges of the pasta together with a fork so that the ravioli is well sealed. Repeat the process until 20 ravioli are made.

In a large pot place the water and bring it to a boil on high heat. Add the salt. Add the ravioli and cook them until they are al dente. Remove the ravioli with a slotted spoon.

On a heated platter place the ravioli. Spoon on the Walnut Cream Sauce. Sprinkle on the Parmesan cheese.

serves 4

"I would describe this dish as 'awesome'! The salmon flavor, which is dominant, combines so deliciously with the more delicate flavor of the Ricotta. And, the Walnut Cream Sauce is the perfect crowning touch."

"Buy the pasta sheets from a pasta shop, or make them from scratch."

"This is not hard to make, although it takes some time, because you are making the ravioli one by one. Actually, it's kind of a soothing recipe to prepare."

"Instead of Parmesan cheese you might want to try Asiago, which is another hard, white Italian cheese. The flavor is richer and stronger than Parmesan."

Walnut Cream Sauce

1	cup walnuts
¼	cup Parmesan cheese, freshly grated
½	cup heavy cream
¼	cup olive oil

In a blender place all of the ingredients and purée them until the mixture is of a creamy consistency.

In a small saucepan pour the sauce. Heat it very slowly on low.

"I try to use the freshest ingredients possible, but without a lot of complicated flavors, because otherwise I will lose the taste of the main ingredient that I am preparing."

Linguini and Bay Scallops in Orange Ginger Cream

4	tablespoons clarified butter
1	teaspoon ginger, freshly grated
¾	pound bay scallops, medium size
¼	cup orange juice, freshly squeezed
2	cups heavy cream
1	pound linguini, cooked al dente

In a large sauté pan place the clarified butter and heat it on medium until it is hot. Add the ginger.

Add the scallops and stir them in.

Add the fresh orange juice and stir it in.

Sauté the scallops until they are just cooked through.

Add the heavy cream and stir it in. Cook the sauce until it is slightly reduced and of a creamy consistency.

Add the linguini and toss it in the sauce so that it is well coated.

serves 4

"I was looking for an interesting way to prepare bay scallops, and because I love ginger and garlic so much, I finally came up with this recipe."

"You can use the orange-ginger combination as a marinade for scallops, or for a light fish or chicken breast. Then just grill them, and this way you will have a lighter dish but with some important tastes."

Pollo Verde

4   **tablespoons flour** *(or as needed)*
½   **teaspoon salt**
¼   **teaspoon pepper**
4   **5-ounce chicken breasts, skin removed, boned, and cubed medium**
4   **tablespoons vegetable oil**
4   **tablespoons dry white wine**
2   **tablespoons butter**
½   **cup heavy cream**
1   **cup zucchini, shredded**
½   **cup cooked green chile peppers, chopped**
¼   **cup piñon nuts** *(or pine nuts)*
    salt *(to taste)*
    white pepper *(to taste)*

In a small bowl place the flour, salt, and pepper. Mix them together.

Dredge the chicken pieces in the flour.

In a large sauté pan place the oil and heat it on medium high until it is hot. Add the floured chicken pieces and sauté them until they are lightly browned.

Add the white wine and deglaze the pan. Reduce the heat to low.

Add the butter and heavy cream, and cook the ingredients for 2 to 3 minutes, or until the liquid is slightly reduced.

Add the zucchini, green chile peppers, and piñon nuts. Cook them until they are just heated through. Add the salt and pepper to taste.

serves 4

"Some years ago I developed this recipe when we needed a sauté dish that was done in a Southwestern style. I experimented quite a bit and found that the zucchini worked really well with the piñon nuts and the green chiles."

"This dish is not overly spicy, because we use the mild green chiles."

"Serve this with your favorite kind of rice. It's excellent!"

Ricotta and Prosciutto Cannelloni

2	tablespoons vegetable oil
¾	cup zucchini, diced
¾	cup mushrooms, diced
1	cup prosciutto, diced
2	cups Ricotta cheese
2	egg yolks
8	7" by 7" pasta sheets, cooked al dente
2	cups heavy cream
2	tablespoons butter
¼	cup Parmesan cheese, freshly grated
½	cup tomatoes, peeled, seeded, and diced
¼	cup fresh basil, chopped

"The prosciutto is the dominant flavor of this dish, and it combines very well with the zucchini and mushrooms. And, the fresh basil and tomatoes in the cream sauce add two more good flavors. All in all, this is a pretty great tasting recipe!"

"This is another one of those dishes that you can serve to almost anyone and they will love it."

In a medium sauté pan place the oil and heat it on medium until it is hot. Add the zucchini and mushrooms, and sauté them for 3 to 4 minutes, or until they are tender.

In a large bowl place the sautéed zucchini and mushrooms, the prosciutto, Ricotta cheese, and egg yolks. Mix the ingredients together well.

On each pasta sheet place a portion of the filling. Roll the pasta up to form a tube.

Place the cannelloni in a baking dish.

In a medium saucepan place the heavy cream, butter, and Parmesan cheese. Heat the ingredients on medium until the liquid is slightly reduced. Add the tomatoes and basil, and stir them in.

Preheat the oven to 350°. Pour the sauce over the cannelloni and bake it for 35 minutes.

serves 4

Ogelvie's Grilled Salmon with Pesto Cream Linguini

Ogelvie's Grilled Salmon

4	7-ounce salmon steaks
⅓	cup olive oil
3	tablespoons fresh basil, chopped
	Pesto Cream Linguini *(recipe on next page)*
4	sprigs fresh basil
1	lemon, quartered

In a shallow pan place the salmon. Drizzle on the olive oil. Sprinkle on the fresh basil. Let the salmon marinate for 2 to 3 hours.

Grill the salmon for 3 to 4 minutes on each side, or until it is just done.

Place the Pesto Cream Linguini on individual, warmed serving plates. Place the salmon steaks next to the linguini.

Garnish the salmon with the basil sprigs and the lemon.

serves 4

"As with any fish, be sure that you don't overcook the salmon, or else it will be too dry."

"You can marinate the salmon with other kinds of fresh herbs, but the basil works particularly well with the Pesto Cream Linguini."

"To me, the visual presentation of food is important, but I also don't like to complicate a dish with a lot of elaborate garnishes. I prefer to present food in its pure state, with the plate looking clean."

*"This is a side dish that
we serve with many
different entrées at the
restaurant. It's also
excellent with other types
of grilled fish or
chicken."*

*"The pesto can be made
ahead of time. It stores
very well, and it should
keep in the refrigerator
for up to two weeks."*

Pesto Cream Linguini

2	**cups fresh basil leaves**
4	**cloves garlic, chopped**
⅛	**cup piñon nuts** *(or pine nuts)*
1	**cup Parmesan cheese, freshly grated**
6	**tablespoons olive oil** *(or as needed)*
½	**cup heavy cream**
1	**pound linguini, cooked al dente**

In a blender place the basil, garlic, piñon nuts, and Parmesan
cheese. Purée the ingredients.

With the blender running, slowly add the olive oil until a
smooth consistency is reached.

In a large sauté pan place the pesto and the heavy cream.
Stir the ingredients together over medium high heat for 2 to 3
minutes, or until the sauce is slightly reduced.

Add the linguini and toss it in so that it is well coated with the
sauce.

150

Grilled Chicken and Vegetable Fettucini

¾   **pound chicken breasts, skin and bones removed**
3   **tablespoons vegetable oil**
2   **cups prepared marinara sauce**
1   **cup broccoli florets, lightly steamed**
1   **cup carrots, sliced and lightly steamed**
½   **cup red bell peppers, sliced and lightly steamed**
1   **pound fettucini, cooked al dente**
     black pepper, freshly ground
½   **cup Parmesan cheese, freshly grated**

Brush the chicken breasts with the oil.

Grill *(or broil)* the chicken for 4 to 5 minutes on each side, or until it is cooked through.

Slice the chicken.

In a large sauté pan place the marinara sauce. Add the sliced chicken, broccoli, carrots, and red bell peppers. Heat the sauce on medium and stir the ingredients together.

Add the fettucini and toss it in so that it is well coated with the sauce, and the vegetables are evenly dispersed.

On 4 individual, heated serving plates place the fettucini. Grind on the black pepper to taste. Sprinkle on the Parmesan cheese.

serves 4

"This is another one of our 'light and healthy' dishes. The marinated chicken has that delicious grilled, herb flavor. And when you mix it with the fresh vegetables and marinara sauce in the fettucini, the result is a unique combination of flavors that most people find very appealing. This is one of our most popular pasta dishes."

"I travel extensively and I love to eat in restaurants. So, I am always picking up ideas from around the country and then bringing them back to New Mexico. I try to incorporate these ideas into our recipes at Ogelvie's to make them more interesting."

Ogelvie's Adobe Pie

<table>
<tr><td>5</td><td>cups chocolate wafers, ground</td></tr>
<tr><td>1</td><td>cup melted butter</td></tr>
<tr><td>4</td><td>tablespoons sugar</td></tr>
<tr><td>3</td><td>cups Häagen Daz coffee ice cream, softened</td></tr>
<tr><td>2</td><td>cups Häagen Daz chocolate ice cream, softened</td></tr>
<tr><td>1</td><td>cup chocolate fudge, melted</td></tr>
<tr><td>3</td><td>cups Häagen Daz coffee ice cream, softened</td></tr>
<tr><td>¼</td><td>cup sliced almonds, toasted</td></tr>
<tr><td>1</td><td>cup heavy cream, whipped</td></tr>
<tr><td>¼</td><td>cup chocolate syrup</td></tr>
<tr><td>8</td><td>chocolate wafer cookies</td></tr>
</table>

In a medium bowl place the ground chocolate wafers, butter, and sugar. Mix the ingredients together well.

Pat the mixture into a 3" deep by 9" wide springform pan so that the bottom and sides are evenly coated.

Preheat the oven to 350°. Bake the pie shell for 5 minutes. Remove the pie shell from the oven, let it cool, and place it in the refrigerator for 1 hour.

Evenly spread the first 3 cups of coffee ice cream in the bottom of the pie shell. Freeze it for 2 hours.

Evenly spread the chocolate ice cream on top, and freeze it for 1 hour.

Evenly spread on the melted chocolate fudge and freeze the pie until it is hard.

Evenly spread on the other 3 cups of coffee ice cream. Sprinkle on the sliced almonds. Freeze the pie for 2 hours.

Remove the springform pan.

Spread on the whipped cream. Dribble on the chocolate syrup.

Cut the pie into 8 wedges. Stick a cookie into the top of each piece.

serves 8

"The Adobe Pie is our signature dessert.....it's the one that we are known for. You could call it chocolate decadence, for sure!"

"Using a top quality ice cream like Häagen Daz makes all the difference. It holds up so well when you soften it and then re-freeze it, not to mention its exquisite taste."

"We've always wanted to find some miniature wooden ladders to lean against the Adobe Pie, but we've never found anyone to make them for us. So, our Adobe Pies are ladderless!"

Gate Detail, Taos, New Mexico

Roberto's

Nestled in a 200-year-old adobe building, Roberto's offers authentic Northern New Mexican d[...] whose secrets have been passed down for many generations. If you wish to experience the "esse[...] of Taos," a visit here is a must!

Menu

*Whole Wheat
Flour Tortillas*

*Taos Chicken
Enchilada Casserole*

Rellenos de Carne

Calabacitas

Sopaipillas

*Gingerbread Coffeehouse
Cookies*

Roberto and Patsy Garcia have run their restaurant since 1965, and they haven't changed their style in all those years.

"This recipe came from Patsy's brother, Dick Valdez, who used to watch their mother make tortillas. And, by a lot of trial and error, he came up with this recipe. The whole wheat flour makes them better, and more nutritious. They are very easy to make!"

Whole Wheat Flour Tortillas

3	cups white flour
1	cup whole wheat flour
2	teaspoons salt
4	teaspoons baking powder
¼	cup lard, warmed to room temperature
1½	cups water, lukewarm

In a medium bowl place the two flours, salt, and baking powder. Mix them together well.

Add the lard and work it in with your hands until pea-size pieces are formed.

Very slowly add the water and work it in with your hands. Knead the dough until it is smooth *(like pie dough)*.

Cover the dough with a wet towel and let it sit for 30 minutes.

Divide the dough into 16 parts and roll them into balls.

On a floured board roll out each dough ball with a rolling pin to form a circle ⅛" thick.

Wipe a skillet with a paper towel dipped in oil. Heat the skillet on medium and cook the tortillas for 1 to 2 minutes on each side, or until brown spots appear.

Serve the tortillas warm.

makes 16 tortillas

chilada Casserole

m soup
up

peppers, diced

neddar cheese, grated
chicken, skin removed, boned,
ubed

medium saucepan place the cream of mushroom soup, cream of chicken soup, water, and green chile peppers. Stir the ingredients together and bring the mixture to a boil. Turn off the heat.

In a large, well-greased casserole dish place 3 of the tortillas in a staggered pattern.

Sprinkle on ¼ of the cheese.

Add ⅓ of the chicken.

Spoon on ⅓ of the soup mixture.

Repeat the process two more times. Stagger the tortillas differently for each layer.

Top the casserole with a layer of the cheese.

Preheat the oven to 350°. Bake the casserole for 1 hour, or until it is hot and bubbly.

serves 8

"This is a relatively modern recipe. Obviously people didn't have Campbell's cream of chicken soup in the old days! I love it because it tastes wonderful, and it's so quick and easy to make. It's a perfect recipe for busy working mothers, or for a party, and it's the kind of dish that everyone enjoys eating. The green chiles are the key to the good flavor."

"The Taos culture is very old and it has developed for over 400 years. So, it has had time to form its own unique essence. If you ask me, 'What is Taos like?' all I can say is, 'Taos is Taos!'"

"Our restaurant is an expression of Taos, and so is the food that we serve. It is very authentic."

Roberto's

Rellenos de Carne

2	pounds roast beef, cooked
1	medium onion, chopped
2	cloves garlic, minced
1	4-ounce can green chile peppers, diced
1	teaspoon salt
4	eggs, well beaten
3	tablespoons oil

Grind the roast beef in a meat grinder *(or chop it in a food processor)*. In a medium bowl place the ground meat, onions, garlic, green chile peppers, and salt. Mix all of the ingredients together until they are well incorporated.

Add the beaten eggs and mix them in well.

In a large skillet place the oil and heat it on medium high until it is hot. Drop in tablespoonfuls of the meat mixture to form 6 patties. Fry them for 2 to 3 minutes on each side, or until the egg is set and they are golden brown.

Repeat the process until all of the mixture is used.

serves 4

Calabacitas

2	tablespoons oil
3	cups green baby pumpkins, diced into ½" squares
½	medium onion, diced
1	can creamed corn
1	4-ounce can green chile peppers, diced
12	Whole Wheat Flour Tortillas, warmed *(see page 153)*

In a large skillet place the oil and heat it on medium until it is hot. Add the diced pumpkin and onions. Sauté the vegetables for 5 to 7 minutes, or until the pumpkin is tender. Add the creamed corn and green chile peppers. Cook the mixture for 10 minutes.

Serve the dish with the Whole Wheat Flour Tortillas.

serves 6

"This is a delicious recipe! It's easy to make and it's a great way to use up your left-over roast beef. Or, you can use any other kind of left-over meat or chicken. It's kind of a variation of chile rellenos, which Roberto's is well known for."

"This recipe, as well as all our others, is typical of Northern New Mexican dishes."

"Calabacitas are the small, green, baby pumpkins which people aren't accustomed to using as a food. Rather, they are used to pumpkins which have already turned orange. Calabacitas are very sweet, and they taste delicious. But since they are so seasonal, people may not be able to find them, so it's perfectly okay to substitute zucchini or yellow squash."

"You can add some cheese to this dish if you want to make it richer."

Sopaipillas

6   **cups flour**
2   **teaspoons baking powder**
2   **teaspoons salt**
2   **tablespoons lard, warmed to room temperature**
1¼ **cups water, lukewarm**
4   **cups lard** (or as needed)
    honey

In a large bowl sift together the flour, baking powder, and salt.

Add the 2 tablespoons of lard and work it in well with your hands.

Slowly add the water and work it in well with your hands. The dough should be smooth (like bread dough).

Cover the dough with a wet towel. Let it sit for 30 minutes at room temperature.

On a floured board roll out the dough to the thickness of a pie crust.

Cut out 4" by 4" squares.

In a large, heavy pot place the 4 cups of lard and heat it to 350°.

Two at a time, drop the dough squares into the pot. Cook them for 30 seconds on each side, or until they are golden brown.

Drain them on paper towels.

Serve the sopaipillas with honey.

makes 36

"We have been working long and hard to come up with the perfect sopaipilla recipe, and this is it!"

"A lot of people think that to make sopaipillas you use two layers of dough, because they are hollow inside. But this isn't true, as you can see by this recipe. When you drop them in the hot fat, they puff up and get hollow. If they don't do this then the dough is too thin. If you have rolled the dough too thick, then you will have a layer of dough in the middle. So, it's probably a good idea to experiment with a small part of the dough at first, just until you get the hang of it."

"Sopaipillas are very Northern New Mexican. We get people from New York, California, and all over the country, who have never heard of them. Even though you squirt honey inside of them so that they are sweet, it is traditional to eat them with the meal, and not after. And, please don't serve them with butter!"

Gingerbread Coffeehouse Cookies

2	cups shortening
1	cup sugar
5	cups flour
1	teaspoon salt
1	teaspoon baking soda
2	teaspoons ginger
1	teaspoon ground cloves
1	teaspoon cinnamon
¾	cup hot coffee
⅔	cup molasses

In a medium bowl place the shortening and sugar, and cream them together.

In a large bowl sift together the flour, salt, baking soda, ginger, cloves, and cinnamon.

Add the creamed shortening and work it in with your hands.

While stirring constantly, slowly add the coffee and molasses. Stir the ingredients together until they are well mixed.

On a floured board roll out the dough until it is ¼" thick.

Cut out pieces with a gingerbread man cookie cutter.

Preheat the oven to 350°. Place the cookies on a cookie sheet and bake them for 10 minutes, or until they are done.

"Years ago Patsy and I had a little A-frame snack bar at the Taos ski area. It was nestled in some trees at the bottom of the beginner's ski lift, and we called it the Gingerbread Coffeehouse. These gingerbread cookies were our most popular item. The little children especially loved to eat them at the end of a day of skiing!"

"The smell alone makes these cookies worth doing! So, be sure to make them even if you don't want to make the gingerbread men, but just want to make little round cookies."

"The food that we serve in the restaurant is what our mothers used to serve us when we were children. It is food that we remember as being good.....it is food that we love!"

Nicho, Blumenschein House, Taos, New Mexico

St. Bernard's

Located at the hub of the famed Taos Ski Valley, the St. Bernard Hotel is described as a "jewel" for lovers of fine dining and great skiing. The gourmet meals are served to the lodge guests with a warm hospitality that makes each person feel pampered and special!

Menu

Cream of Pumpkin Soup

Fresh Tomato Soup with Basil

Asparagus aux Fines Herbes Vinaigrette

Carottes Glacés

Gratin Dauphinois

Ratatouille

Braised Veal with Oranges

Sea Bass in Tomato Butter Sauce

Tournedos Poivre-Vert

Poulet Sauté à la Basquaise

Blanquette of Veal

Chocolate Soufflé

Tarte aux Framboises

French-born Claude Gohard has been the chef at the Hotel St. Bernard for 20 years. He is a master at blending classic European tastes with those of the Southwest. About this recipe he says, *"Pumpkins are popular both in France and New Mexico."*

Cream of Pumpkin Soup

4	tablespoons butter
2¼	pounds fresh pumpkin, peeled, seeded, and cubed
3	onions, cubed
4	large tomatoes, peeled and cubed
	salt *(to taste)*
	pepper *(to taste)*
5	cups chicken broth
½	cup half and half
1	teaspoon butter

In a large saucepan place the 4 tablespoons of butter and heat it on medium until it has melted. Add the pumpkin and onions, and quickly sauté them until they are well coated with the butter.

Add the tomatoes, salt, pepper, and chicken broth. Stir the ingredients together. Bring the soup to a boil and then simmer it for 40 minutes.

Purée the soup in a blender and then return it to the saucepan.

In a small saucepan place the half and half and bring it to a boil. Add it to the puréed soup and stir it in.

Boil the soup for five minutes. Add the 1 teaspoon of butter and stir it in.

serves 4

Fresh Tomato Soup with Basil

1	tablespoon olive oil
1	carrot, sliced
½	leek, sliced
1	shallot, sliced
3	tomatoes, peeled and chopped
1	tablespoon tomato paste
5	cups chicken stock
1	sprig thyme
1	bay leaf
	salt *(to taste)*
	pepper *(to taste)*
1	teaspoon fresh basil, chopped
1	teaspoon olive oil

In a medium large saucepan place the 1 tablespoon of olive oil and heat it on medium until it is hot. Add the carrots, leeks, and shallots. Shake the vegetables over the heat for 5 minutes.

Add the tomatoes, tomato paste, chicken stock, thyme, bay leaf, salt, and pepper. Stir the ingredients together and simmer them for 20 minutes.

Remove the sprig of thyme and the bay leaf.

In a food processor place the basil and purée it. With the processor still running dribble in the 1 teaspoon of olive oil.

Bring the soup to a boil. Add the puréed basil and stir it in.

serves 4

"The purpose of cooking the vegetables in the oil and shaking them in the pot at the beginning of the recipe is to release their flavors. This is called 'sweating' the vegetables. You should always do this with vegetables that are used in a sauce or soup because then the sugar from them will come out."

"A trick that I like to do is to add a teaspoon of butter to my soups or sauces at the very end, just before I serve them. I just drop it in and stir it around. The flavor of the butter is very rich and fresh tasting because it has not cooked at all."

"Many people do not add the correct amount of salt when they make a vinaigrette, before they add the oil. They complete the recipe, taste it, and then add more salt at the very end. However, if you add more salt at this point then the salt crystals get coated with the oil and they do not readily dissolve, so you do not taste them. The point is, if you have already completed making the dressing and you decide that it needs more salt, then mix the salt with a little water or vinegar and melt it over the heat. Now you can add it to the dressing and you will taste it."

"This vinaigrette is excellent with many vegetables other than asparagus."

"In our basic dinner salad we dress it in the most simple way.....with an excellent vinegar, oil, salt, and pepper."

Asparagus aux Fines Herbes Vinaigrette

1   **hard-boiled egg yolk**
1   **tablespoon Dijon mustard**
1   **teaspoon wine vinegar**
    salt *(to taste)*
    pepper *(to taste)*
1   **cup olive oil**
1   **tablespoon fresh tarragon, finely chopped**
1   **tablespoon fresh parsley, finely chopped**
1   **tablespoon fresh chives, finely chopped**
1   **tablespoon fresh chervil, finely chopped**
32   **asparagus spears, tough ends removed, and steamed**
2   **hard-boiled egg whites, finely chopped**

In a food processor place the hard-boiled egg yolk, Dijon mustard, wine vinegar, salt, and pepper. Purée the ingredients together.

With the food processor still running, slowly pour in the olive oil.

Add the fresh herbs and stir them in.

Pour the vinaigrette on the asparagus. Sprinkle on the chopped egg whites.

serves 4

Carottes Glacés

12 medium carrots, peeled and cut into 2"
   long cylinders
1½ cups chicken stock
4 tablespoons butter
2 tablespoons sugar
½ teaspoon salt
⅛ teaspoon white pepper
2 tablespoons parsley, chopped

In a large skillet place the carrots, chicken stock, butter, sugar, salt, and white pepper. Mix the ingredients together. Cover the skillet and simmer the ingredients for 20 minutes, or until the carrots are just tender. Occasionally shake the skillet.

Remove the carrots with a slotted spoon and set them aside.

Cook the liquid until it is reduced and is of a syrupy consistency.

Add the carrots and roll them in the glaze.

Sprinkle on the parsley.

serves 6

"This is a very simple, but delicious recipe. It also is quite healthy, especially if you cut down on the amount of butter you use, or else substitute oil for the butter."

"I think that simple is best, especially if you can find very fresh vegetables, because they already taste good without doing anything to them."

"You may substitute one tablespoon of honey for the two tablespoons of sugar. Often I will substitute honey for sugar, not only because of the flavor, but because honey is healthier for you. Also, I am a bee keeper! I have three hives, and I use everything that the bees produce. I eat the pollen, I use the wax on my wood floors, and, of course, I use the honey in my cooking."

*"This dish comes from
Grenoble, France, where
the winter Olympics have
been held. All of the
people in this region think
that their own personal
recipe is the very best,
and they all claim that
their recipe is the original
one. So, I am not going to
argue with anyone about
my recipe! But, I must
admit that the best tasting
Gratin Dauphinois that I
ever had was at a farm in
France, where all of the
ingredients were locally
fresh."*

*"Be careful that the
potatoes don't get too
brown before they are
cooked through. This is
why I have you reduce the
heat after fifteen minutes.
You must experiment with
your own oven at your
particular altitude."*

Gratin Dauphinois

3¼ **cups milk, boiling**
1   **egg, slightly beaten**
⅓   **cup Gruyère cheese, grated**
2   **teaspoons garlic, minced**
     salt *(to taste)*
     pepper *(to taste)*
¼   **teaspoon nutmeg, freshly ground**
2   **pounds potatoes, peeled and thinly sliced**
1   **tablespoon butter, melted**
2   **tablespoons Gruyère cheese, grated**

In a medium bowl place the boiling milk, egg, the ⅓ cup of Gruyère cheese, the garlic, salt, pepper, and nutmeg. Mix the ingredients together.

Add the sliced potatoes and mix them in well.

In a well-buttered baking dish place the potato mixture. Dribble on the melted butter. Sprinkle the 2 tablespoons of Gruyère cheese on top.

Preheat the oven to 375°. Bake the potatoes for 15 minutes and then reduce the heat to 325°. Bake the potatoes for 15 to 20 minutes, or until they are very tender.

serves 4

Ratatouille

2 pounds eggplant, peeled and cubed medium
1 tablespoon salt
½ cup olive oil
2 pounds zucchini, cubed medium
¾ pound green bell peppers, seeded and cut into
1" squares
3 cups onions, cubed medium
3 pounds tomatoes, peeled and quartered
2 teaspoons garlic, finely chopped
2 tablespoons fresh basil, chopped
salt *(to taste)*
pepper *(to taste)*

In a colander place the eggplant and sprinkle on the 1 tablespoon of salt. Let the eggplant sit for 30 minutes so that the liquid drains out.

In a large, heavy saucepan place the oil and heat it on medium high until it is hot. Add the eggplant and sauté it for 15 minutes, or until it is lightly browned.

Add the zucchini and sauté it for 2 to 3 minutes. Drain out part of the juice.

Add the bell peppers, onions, tomatoes, garlic, basil, salt, and pepper. Slowly cook the vegetables for 40 minutes.

serves 4

"Here is a wonderful vegetable recipe that you can serve as an entrée or as a side dish. It's good served hot, and I especially love it cold. It also is delicious as a stuffing for an omelette."

"I recommend that you use the Japanese eggplant instead of the larger ones. It always is preferable to use the finest ingredients that you can find, and in this case the Japanese eggplant is much more tender and tasty."

Braised Veal with Oranges

"The flavor of the orange and lemon with the veal is very lovely. This is a beautiful dish and it can be served at an elegant, sophisticated dinner party, or just as a family dish."

1	**5-pound veal roast, cut from heel round of leg**
1	**large onion, thinly sliced**
2	**oranges, juiced**
1	**lemon, juiced**
1	**tablespoon parsley, chopped**
½	**teaspoon thyme**
1	**bay leaf**
	salt *(to taste)*
	pepper *(to taste)*
2	**tablespoons olive oil**
½	**cup chicken broth**
¼	**cup red vinegar**
1	**tablespoon honey**
1	**orange**

In a large pan place the veal, onions, orange juice, lemon juice, parsley, thyme, bay leaf, salt, and pepper. Let the veal marinate for 12 hours. Turn the veal occasionally. Remove the veal and reserve the marinade.

In a roasting pan place the olive oil and heat it on top of the stove until it is hot. Place the veal in the pan and brown it on all sides.

Preheat the oven the 425°. Pour the marinade over the veal. Roast the veal for 1¾ hours, or until it is done.

Remove the veal and the bay leaf. Add the chicken broth to the pan. Pour the liquid into a food processor and blend it. Strain the liquid through a fine sieve.

In a medium saucepan place the vinegar and honey, and bring them to a boil so that the honey is melted. Add the strained liquid to the vinegar and honey, and stir it in.

Peel off the zest *(the thin, orange, outer skin)* of the orange. Blanch the orange zest in boiling water. Carefully cut out the sections of the orange so that there are no white membranes.

Slice the veal and pour on the sauce. Garnish the veal with the orange zest and wedges.

serves 4

Sea Bass in Tomato Butter Sauce

1	tablespoon unsalted butter
4	shallots, chopped
¼	cup white wine
1	tablespoon dry vermouth
¼	cup fish stock
4	ripe tomatoes, peeled and chopped
1	bunch fresh basil
3	tablespoons butter
	salt *(to taste)*
	pepper *(to taste)*
2	pounds sea bass fillets

In a medium sauté pan place the 1 tablespoon of butter and heat it on medium high until it has melted. Add the shallots and sauté them for 2 to 3 minutes, or until they are soft.

Add the wine and vermouth, and bring them to a boil.

Add the fish stock, tomatoes, and 4 basil leaves. Simmer the ingredients for 15 minutes.

Place the mixture in a blender and purée it. Strain the purée through a fine sieve and return it to the sauté pan.

Heat the purée on medium until it is reduced to ⅓. Add the 3 tablespoons of butter, salt, and pepper. Stir them in. Keep the sauce warm.

Place the sea bass in a steamer. Place one basil leaf on top of each fillet. Steam the fish for 7 to 9 minutes, or until it is just done. Remove the basil leaves.

Spoon the Tomato Butter Sauce onto a warmed serving platter. Place the steamed fish on top of the sauce. Garnish the dish with the remainder of the basil leaves.

serves 4

"The sauce must be made first, because as soon as the fish is cooked you should be ready to serve it. You won't have time to make the sauce while the fish is steaming."

"You can use this recipe for any kind of fish. Another way to cook the fish is to wrap it in some foil with some butter and wine, and then bake it."

"The flavor of the basil leaves comes through when you steam them with the fish. But, they won't look too good, so that is why you must discard them and then garnish the fish with fresh leaves."

"My Sous Chef, Isao Kosaka, and I more or less developed this recipe, although its origins are in France."

Tournedos Poivre-Vert

4	6-ounce tournedos of beef
¼	cup cognac
2	tablespoons butter
2	shallots, chopped
½	cup heavy cream
2	teaspoons green peppercorns
	salt *(to taste)*

In a medium bowl place the tournedos and the cognac. Marinate them for 1 hour. *(Save the cognac.)*

In a large sauté pan place the butter and heat it on medium until it has melted. Add the shallots and gently sauté them for 1 to 2 minutes.

Add the tournedos and sauté them on each side until the desired doneness is achieved.

Add the remaining cognac and the cream, and stir them in.

Add the green peppercorns and the salt, and stir them in.

Remove the tournedos and immediately pour the sauce from the pan over them.

serves 4

"Ask your butcher to prepare the tournedos for you."

"Our guests come for one week of pleasure. If we can match good snow with good food, then we will have provided them with the week of their dreams! All of our staff tries to make each person feel very special. Sometimes people will go back into the kitchen and request certain things, and we always try to accommodate them."

"The owner of the St. Bernard, Jean Mayer, is the host for all three meals, every single day. He also is the Technical Director of the Taos Valley Ski School."

Poulet Sauté à la Basquaise

4	tablespoons olive oil
1	2½-pound chicken, cut into 8 pieces
4	tablespoons flour
1	teaspoon garlic, minced
¾	cup mushrooms, sliced
4	medium tomatoes, peeled and diced
4	green bell peppers, seeded and diced
6	ounces prosciutto, diced
2	cups dry white wine
1	cup chicken stock
	salt (to taste)
	pepper (to taste)
1	tablespoon parsley, finely chopped

In a large saucepan place the olive oil and heat it on medium until it is hot. Add the chicken pieces and sauté them until they are golden brown. Remove the chicken and set it aside.

Add the flour to the olive oil and whisk it in to make a roux.

Add the garlic, mushrooms, tomatoes, bell peppers, prosciutto, white wine, chicken stock, salt, pepper, and parsley. Stir the ingredients together.

Add the chicken and simmer it for 20 minutes, or until it is done.

serves 4

"This recipe comes from the Basque country in the Pyrenees Mountains between Spain and France. I used to work there in a ski resort."

"Don't overcook the chicken! Keep checking it and poke it with your fingers to see how it feels."

"I personally like to save the fat from the duck, goose, or chicken that I cook, and then use it instead of butter in my cooking. The flavor is good, and fat won't go bad if you get it too hot, whereas with butter, you can absolutely ruin it if you burn it!"

Blanquette of Veal

2	**pounds veal, fat removed, and cubed medium**
1	**carrot, chopped**
1	**celery stalk, chopped**
1	**cup pearl onions**
1	**bay leaf**
1	**sprig thyme**
2	**cloves garlic**
	salt *(to taste)*
	pepper *(to taste)*
¼	**cup butter**
¼	**cup flour**
½	**pound mushrooms, quartered**
2	**egg yolks**
¼	**cup cream**
½	**lemon, juiced**

In a medium large saucepan place the veal. Cover it with water and bring it to a boil. Drain the veal, rinse it, and place it back in the pot. Cover the veal with fresh water.

Add the carrots, celery, pearl onions, bay leaf, sprig of thyme, garlic, salt, and pepper. Simmer the veal for 20 minutes. Remove the pearl onions and set them aside. Simmer the veal for 1½ hours, or until it is very tender. Remove the veal and strain the broth.

In another medium large saucepan place the butter and heat it on medium until it has melted. Add the flour and whisk it for 2 to 3 minutes. While stirring constantly, add 3 cups of the veal broth. Cook it for 3 to 5 minutes, or until the sauce thickens.

Add the veal, pearl onions, and mushrooms to the sauce.

In a small bowl place the egg yolks and cream, and beat them together. Add the yolk and cream mixture to the veal stew, and stir it in *(do not boil the sauce after this addition)*.

Add the lemon juice and correct the seasoning.

serves 8

"Some people might call this a veal stew. I don't like the word 'stew' for this recipe because it doesn't convey the elegance and special quality of the dish."

"I love this veal.....it is really different tasting! It's not too popular in American restaurants, but in France you can find it anywhere."

"This is a very rich dish, but you can cut down on the amount of cream and butter that you use."

"My only advice is to pay close attention to this recipe. Read it through several times to make certain that you understand it."

Chocolate Soufflé

4	tablespoons sugar
6	ounces unsweetened chocolate
9	egg yolks
15	egg whites
4	tablespoons sugar
1	tablespoon sugar

In the top of a simmering double boiler place the first 4 tablespoons of sugar and the unsweetened chocolate. Heat the chocolate until it has melted. Remove the pan from the heat.

Add the egg yolks and beat them in.

In a medium bowl place the egg whites and the other 4 tablespoons of sugar and beat them until soft peaks are formed. Fold the egg whites into the melted chocolate.

In a well-buttered mold sprinkle in the 1 tablespoon of sugar. Pour in the soufflé mixture so that it comes almost to the rim.

Preheat the oven to 425°. Place the mold in a baking dish that is half filled with hot water. Place it in the oven and then reduce the heat to 325°. Bake the soufflé for 15 to 20 minutes, or until it is done.

serves 4

"To make a soufflé is not as difficult to do as everyone thinks. The only problem is that you have to synchronize making it with serving and eating your dinner. Sometimes this is difficult, especially if you are the host or hostess with dinner guests, because you probably are busy with other aspects of preparing the meal."

"This soufflé goes very well with a Crème Anglaise (white vanilla sauce). I like to boil the milk with some fresh mint, and then strain it. This adds a nice subtle flavor to the sauce."

Tarte aux Framboises

2	egg yolks
6	tablespoons sugar
⅔	cup butter
¾	cup flour
5	egg yolks
1	drop vanilla
2	tablespoons sugar
¼	cup flour
2	cups milk, heated
2	pounds raspberries, washed and stems removed
¼	cup currant jelly, melted

"To make the dough is very simple.....just mix the ingredients together. Also, you can make it one day ahead of time."

In a medium bowl place the 2 egg yolks, the 6 tablespoons of sugar, the butter, and the ¾ cup of flour. Mix the ingredients together well to form a dough.

Roll out the dough and fit it into a tart pan. Place a piece of parchment paper on the dough and fill it up with dried beans.

"One trick that I like to do is to brush some melted chocolate on the bottom of the cooked tart shell, and then let it harden. This way the dough won't get soft when you pour on the custard.... it will stay nice and crispy."

Preheat the oven to 325°. Bake the tart shell for 20 to 30 minutes, or until it is lightly browned. Let the shell cool. Remove the dried beans and the parchment paper.

In a medium saucepan place the 5 egg yolks, the vanilla, the 2 tablespoons of sugar, and the ¼ cup of flour. Beat the ingredients together. Add the heated milk and mix it in. While stirring constantly, heat the mixture until it comes to a boil.

Let the custard sit for 20 minutes.

"I like to add one tablespoon of almond powder to the dough. By doing so, a delicious, subtle flavor is achieved."

Pour the custard into the tart shell. Place the raspberries on top. Brush on the melted currant jelly.

Serve the tart cool *(do not refrigerate)*.

serves 6

"You also can use strawberries in this recipe, or other kinds of fruits that are in season."

Supplemental Information

Mail order catalogues, or information about ordering special Southwestern ingredients, may be obtained from the following sources:

The Chile Shop
109 East Water Street
Santa Fe, NM 87501

(505) 983-6080

Gift N' Gourmet
55 Old Santa Fe Trail
Santa Fe, NM 87501

(505) 982-5953

Santa Fe Chile Line
2565 Camino San Patricio
Santa Fe, NM 87505

(505) 983-1322

Index

COOKBOOK ORDER FORMS

Please send me a total of _____ copy(ies) of *Taos Recipe* at $11.95 each, and/or _____ copy(ies) of *Santa Fe Recipe** at $13.95 each. I am enclosing $2.50 for shipping and handling charges for the first book, and $1.50 for each additional book.

Taos Recipe Total _____

Santa Fe Recipe Total _____

Shipping and Handling Total _____

NM residents please enclose $.68 per *Taos Recipe*, and $.79 per *Santa Fe Recipe*, sales tax _____

Total Amount Enclosed _____

Ship to _____

Address _____

City _____

State _____ Zip _____

Make check or money order payable to
Tierra Publications

Mail to:

Tierra Publications
2801 Rodeo Road, Suite B-612
Santa Fe, New Mexico 87505

Please send me a total of _____ copy(ies) of *Taos Recipe* at $11.95 each, and/or _____ copy(ies) of *Santa Fe Recipe** at $13.95 each. I am enclosing $2.50 for shipping and handling charges for the first book, and $1.50 for each additional book.

Taos Recipe Total _____

Santa Fe Recipe Total _____

Shipping and Handling Total _____

NM residents please enclose $.68 per *Taos Recipe*, and $.79 per *Santa Fe Recipe*, sales tax _____

Total Amount Enclosed _____

Ship to _____

Address _____

City _____

State _____ Zip _____

Make check or money order payable to
Tierra Publications

Mail to:

Tierra Publications
2801 Rodeo Road, Suite B-612
Santa Fe, New Mexico 87505

* *Santa Fe Recipe* "A Cookbook of Recipes from Favorite Local Restaurants" · 300 recipes · 30 restaurants · 305 pages.